Decorating
on a
Shoestring

Decorating on a Shoestring

You Can Create a Beautiful Home Without Spending a Fortune

GWEN ELLIS & JO ANN JANSSEN

BROADMAN
& HOLMAN
PUBLISHERS

Nashville, Tennessee

© 1999 by Jo Ann Janssen and Gwen Ellis
All rights reserved
Printed in the United States of America

0-8054-1773-7

Published by Broadman & Holman Publishers, Nashville, Tennessee
Editorial Team: Vicki Crumpton, Janis Whipple, Kim Overcash
Interior Design and Art Direction: Paul T. Gant, Art & Design
Typesetting: SL Editorial Services
Illustrations: Jim Osborn
Cover Design: Steve Diggs and Friends
Cover Photography: Jerry Atnip

Dewey Decimal Classification: 645
Subject Heading: HOUSE FURNISHINGS/INTERIOR DECORATION
Library of Congress Card Catalog Number: 98-41079

All Scripture used is taken from the NKJV, New King James Version, copyright © 1979, 1980, 1982, Thomas Nelson, Inc., Publishers.

Library of Congress Cataloging-in-Publication Data

Ellis, Gwen, 1938–
    Decorating on a shoestring / Gwen Ellis, Jo Ann Janssen.
       p. cm.
    ISBN 0-8054-1773-7 (pbk.)
    1. House furnishings. 2. Interior decoration. 3. Consumer education.   I. Janssen, Jo Ann,
    1952– . II. Title.
    TX311.E47   1999
    645—dc21

                                        98-41079
                                         CIP

1 2 3 4 5 03 02 01 00 99

Dedication

I dedicate this book to my husband, Al. You encouraged me to pursue my interest in interior decorating. You have believed in me and been my best advisor throughout the writing of this book. I couldn't have, and wouldn't have, done it without you.

Jo

To Judy Couchman who first planted the seed for this book in my mind.

To Al Janssen who believed in this project, critiqued and edited the book, acted as agent, and loaned me his wife as cowriter.

And to my niece, Karen Vanderweide, who has become the queen of shoestring decorating.

Gwen

Table of Contents

Acknowledgments

A first time author needs a great deal of professional help! My thanks and admiration go to all the gracious and patient people at Broadman & Holman, especially to Dr. Vicki Crumpton and Janis Whipple who kindly answered all my questions and pulled this whole thing together rather nicely. My thanks and admiration for their abilities go to the artists, Paul Gant and Jim Osborn, who designed and illustrated this book. Their drawings beautifully complimented our words.

The prayers and encouragement from my friends were invaluable. Thank you women at Woodmen Valley Chapel, MIT prayer warriors, Dewsbury friends, Vickie Howard, and my extended family in Phoenix.

Finally I must acknowledge my husband, Al, and children, Joshua, Jonathan, and Anna. It is one thing to patiently live through many decorating projects and experiments over the years. They deserve some kind of award for living with me while writing this book. Thank you guys for believing in me and putting up with me.

Jo

Thanks to Vicki Crumpton for saying yes to our idea and for shepherding the book through all its processes.

Thanks to Janis Whipple for the editorial process you've taken this book through to make it not just a good book, but a great book.

Thanks designers and artists for giving the book a fresh, upbeat look.

Thanks JoAnn for your patience as I moved twice during the writing of this book, started a new job, and redecorated a house while trying to write. You've been a great friend and a wonderful collaborator.

Thanks Janssen kids for sharing your parents with me during the writing of this book. I love you all.

Gwen

FOREWORD

Decorating on a Shoestring

If you've been living under the assumption that you need loads of money to have a beautifully decorated home, forget it. It's not money that you need—it's ideas! *In Decorating on a Shoestring*, Jo Ann Janssen and Gwen Ellis offer hundreds of the most clever and creative ideas for how to use the things you already have—or can get for a song—to create the look you love most.

I'll admit it. I was a bit skeptical before reading this book. Sure I'm thrifty—even call myself a cheapskate—but I'm not into tacky. I have a fairly high standard for the way I want my home to look and feel, and while I'm certainly not going into debt to accomplish it, neither am I willing to sink to a new level of shabbiness.

I breathed my first sigh of relief when I read principle #2 on page 6: Acquire the best quality furnishings possible. These women speak my language! Once I knew they would not be recommending inferior material, construction or designs, anything fake or plastic, particle board or other faddish items, I was hooked.

Convinced that color, mood, and style can significantly impact the way we feel in our homes and interact with our families, I'm all revved up to get going on a few home decorating improvement projects myself. As soon as I find a stack of books like Gwen describes in chapter 5, page 44—the kind no one could pay you to read but with nice bindings in attractive colors—an ugly, albeit useful, lamp that's currently stashed in a closet will be undergoing a serious makeover. And I cannot wait to stop by the Drapery Workroom in my city to see if they have any "goofs" (chapter 7, page 60) or bolt ends of fabric I might be able to use to perk up our master bedroom windows. What a great idea!

I am so grateful to the authors for writing such a useful book. Now if they'd just get busy with a companion volume that will help create a little more time in my day, I'll be all set!

Mary Hunt
Editor, *Cheapskate Monthly*
Author, *The Financially Confident Woman*, *Debt-Proof Your Kids*, and *Tiptionary*

Introduction

We, Jo and Gwen, love to decorate our homes. We like to dream, plan, shop, look at decorating books and magazines, rearrange, paint, and sew—anything having to do with interior decorating. The whole process of creating beautiful homes gives us much satisfaction. Living in the homes we have created brings joy to us, to our families, and to our guests as well.

Someday, in the sweet by and by, when we reach our final address on Golden Street, Heaven, we will have perfect homes. We will have mansions prepared especially for us! They will be perfectly decorated, heavenly comfortable, just the right size, and pleasing in every way. But in the meantime, here on earth we will need to use our God-given abilities to create as much beauty in our homes as possible.

Every principle and idea for making a lovely home can be found in God's creation. There we find the colors, contrasts, composition, and harmony to create beauty and comfort. When we talk about a "rainbow of colors" we all have a visual picture of something beautiful God made. When we talk about "feathering a nest" we get a sense of great comfort. What we need to learn is how to translate these principles of God's creation into our homes while staying within our shoestring budgets.

We want to help you get from where you are in your home decorating to where you'd like to be. None of us has God's ability to speak perfect and beautiful things into existence. It's going to take work and experimentation for us mere humans to create beauty. We have had a lot of practice decorating our homes on a shoestring budget.

Gwen's Story

Gwen was a pastor's wife for a long time. When she looks back, she wonders how they existed on their meager salary at their first church. Miraculously, though, they were able to purchase a house. It had all white interior walls and cathedral ceilings throughout. It was a small house but those high ceilings helped give an illusion of space.

Paint, mill end fabrics a man sold out of his garage, some never-used shutters Gwen found at a garage sale, some construction with lumber scraps, and some bargain and hand-me-down furniture all added up to a lovely home where they did a lot of entertaining.

Their next house was in Seattle, where Gwen spent fifteen years transforming a drab 70s contemporary-styled house into a European country-styled home. The result was a charming place that sold for four times what they paid for it.

Then Gwen's life changed drastically and she found herself moving to Colorado Springs alone. While waiting for her ideal house to be constructed, she dreamed, picked out fabrics, chose the tile for kitchen and bathroom, and watched thrift shops for just the right furniture pieces.

It all came together beautifully, but Gwen was only able to enjoy it for three years before more drastic changes came along. Gwen became ill with cancer and after a hard fight, beat the disease just in time to accept a new position in Michigan, where she is now doing her shoestring decorating magic on a new (old, dated) house.

Jo's Story

Jo, unlike Gwen, always said she would never marry a pastor because she didn't want to be poor. So she married Al, a poor writer, instead! Jo taught school for eight years to save up enough money to buy their first little cottage just months before baby Joshua arrived. Not knowing when or how much money there was going to be, Jo had to do a lot with what she had. She switched around or remade the existing curtains and painted all the rooms. Friends lent them nursery furniture. Jo carefully arranged her refinished yard sale finds. A cute cottage-style home was the result.

After six years and one more son, they moved from their Salem cottage into a small ranch-styled home near Portland, Oregon. With a daughter about to arrive, Jo got busy. She painted again and taught herself to stencil the walls. She sewed curtains and made bookshelves, and when she went to replace the ugly linoleum, she discovered some wonderful oak flooring and had it refinished.

Jo was almost done with the house when the Janssens moved to Colorado Springs. There they bought a large two-story ugly duckling. Transforming the dark 70s-style house into a light and bright contemporary country-styled home required new carpeting, wood floors, and curtains. Jo applied many, many gallons of white paint to cover the dark doors, stair railings, and trim. She did more stenciling and even painted a garden mural in the powder room. With her decorating magic done, the house is now on the market. Jo wants something smaller and she's ready for a new decorating challenge.

The Lord has put both of us in different, but always shoestring budget, circumstances. We've lived in many styles and sizes of houses. Sometimes we had a little money to spend but usually we had none. We tried to be content like the apostle Paul in "whatever state" we are in. (Philippians 4:11–12, NKJV). We kept reminding ourselves of Hebrews 13:5 to "be content with such things as you have" (NKJV).

Well, maybe we weren't perfectly content! We always tried to improve our homes to increase their beauty, functionality, and value. We used all the resources God gave us. Sometimes all we had was creativity, imagination, and a few dried weeds from a nearby park to begin our decorating. Our shoestring budgets were that tight! But going into debt to decorate our homes was never an option. We couldn't afford it! Sometimes God dropped blessings in our laps: helpful friends, hand-me-down furniture, dumpster finds, and incredible buys were some of our gifts. God always knew our needs and met them in many ways. We have lots of examples of that provision throughout this book.

Besides figuring out how to make something from nothing and waiting for God to meet our needs, we also figured out how to do things for ourselves. Sometimes God's gifts required a little mending, painting, and refinishing. We figured out how to do those things and many more. It seems we always had more time, imagination, patience, and perseverance than we had money. Figuring out how to do things ourselves has become a habit that we couldn't break even if we were to become wealthy. (Although we wouldn't mind trying that for a while!)

Making our homes into refuges of peace and beauty is important to us. Even Jesus needed a quiet place to rejuvenate at the end of each day. Everyone has a different idea of what it takes to make a house meet this need. We will help you figure that out for your family so your home will also be a refuge that gives you satisfaction and joy.

Our homes are not only our refuges, they are also an extension of who we are. We like them to reflect our tastes, styles, interest, and personalities. Since every one of us is one of God's unique creations, each of our homes will be uniquely ours as well. The people in our homes keep growing, learning about new things, and having new needs. These changes in tastes, needs, and interests will be reflected by changes in our homes. It seems our homes are never really done. We are always finding ways to improve them.

It is our desire to motivate you to use your God-given abilities (whether undeveloped, latent, or well-hidden) and the resources He has given you to create the most beautiful and functional home you can. It will take time. It may entail a lot of work. But we believe that with your resources, abilities, and the help we provide in this book, you can decorate your home beautifully on a shoestring.

CHAPTER 1

We've Been There—Done That

Home. We want it to look like something in *House Beautiful*. But we want to spend on a *Cheapskate Monthly* budget.

"Can't be done!" you say. We believe it can. In fact, we have done it and are doing it. It takes work, patience, and creativity, but your family and friends can feel comfortable and welcome in a well-decorated home. And all on a shoestring.

We can hear the roar already. "I don't know how to do it and besides, I doubt if anyone in my family would even notice." "Decorating costs lots of money and I can't afford it." "I have kids." "I have pets."

Add to that the pressure of conforming to all the unrealistic models around us. There is Martha Stewart and her television programs. There's *Country Living, Metropolitan Homes,* and *Traditional Homes* magazines. Homes in these magazines look so wonderful and beautiful, but all of that information can be intimidating, especially since a good deal of the decorating ideas are also very complicated and expensive.

Hmmm. Sounds to us like you could use some help and encouragement. That's why we've written this book and named it *Decorating on a Shoestring*. Even if you only have one shoestring and it's frayed or broken, we'll show you how to make your home more charming, using what you have. And if you can add just a little fabric, paint, and elbow grease, we'll show you how to turn your home into one that family, friends, and neighbors enjoy and tell others about. It *can* be done and done inexpensively. We promise!

We (your authors) are at different stages in our lives. Jo is the wife of a very busy man and has three children at home. Her lifestyle includes school and church activities, lots of entertaining, serving as taxi driver for all three of her kids, and all the other normal functions of a typical American family where everyone is still living under one roof.

Gwen has experienced that great, once-in-a-lifetime happening, the emancipation of her children. Her lifestyle has changed drastically over the last few years, and she now lives alone except for two black and white cats named Charles Dickens and Tiny Tim. (Well, what did you expect from a writer?)

Between the two of us, we've experienced most of the situations you face. Frankly, neither one of us has ever had much money for decorating. We've learned a few things about taking what we have and making it work. We've learned sources for getting the things we didn't have. And we've learned that hard work often makes up for a lack of funds.

Both of us enjoy the business, planning, and sense of accomplishment that comes with doing a decorating project. We care about the finished product, too, but we see it as a challenge to save as much money as possible getting there.

Throughout the book, we'll tell you some of our stories to illustrate that you can successfully decorate your home without spending a fortune. But first, we need to give you the philosophy by which we do this. We've identified six basic principles that undergird this book. There will be many tips and how-to's throughout sixteen chapters, but these six principles—two about decorating and four dealing with attitude—will reappear throughout the book. Technique is part of making a nice home. But attitude is everything. So here are six starting points.

PRINCIPLE #1:
Create a Unifying Element in Every Room

People often ask Gwen how things always look as if they belong together, no matter how she puts them together or which rooms she uses them in. Her answer: "I use two basic colors—red and blue—for everything in my house. There are several shades of blue—everything from navy to Wedgewood to blue-green, and I use several shades of red—everything from barn red to pink. It means that most of my furnishings are interchangeable throughout the house. It works for me."

Jo builds her rooms around books, the colors of blue and white with red accents, and gardening themes.

Every room needs a unifying element. You can do this with style, ambiance, color, motifs, and themes. A room that looks as if its elements fit with each other is a more unified, comfortable, and well-decorated room. We will help you think through and discover what it is you really like, need, and want in your rooms so you can pull everything together with great style.

PRINCIPLE #2:
Acquire the Best Quality Furnishings Possible

This may sound like a contradiction, given that this book is about decorating on a low budget. But quality will save you money in the long term. We have made the mistake of buying cheap so we could have it now. Eventually, we were always sorry we spent our hard-earned money on something that looked junky a year or two later. It is better to do without than to live with junk. You will have to do some research, learn what real quality is, and wait until you can afford it. We will teach you how and where to find quality things at prices that are more realistic for your budget than what you can find at a furniture store.

There are some things that will never look good because of their inferior materials, construction, or designs. Anything fake or plastic falls into that category. Particle board, laminated surfaces that are supposed to look like wood, fake matting on framed prints, thin fabric, faddish items, and things that don't weigh as much as their higher quality counterparts are all examples of second-rate junk you want to get rid of or avoid.

PRINCIPLE #3:
Think Creatively

This is the first of four invaluable attitudes. You will discover that we don't always look at objects the way they were intended to be used. We often look for something that will function for a particular purpose and have certain dimensions. So we might find those qualities in an unexpected object or place. We first try to use what we already have so no expenditure is needed. We keep our eyes and minds open.

For example, Jo's first nursery included a changing table made from stackable storage units that she painted to look like wood. In their previous life they had served as an entertainment center, and then as a desk, placed on end and topped with an old door to make a large work surface. By stacking one on top of the other, they served a new purpose—they were just the right height for a changing table. "I purchased a piece of foam rubber to fit the top and covered it with a printed plastic available by the yard at fabric stores. For pennies, we had a changing table that matched the decor of the room. Later, those same units became toy storage for our sons, Joshua and Jonathan, and today are in our daughter Anna's closet as low storage shelves."

Gwen's family room coffee table is big enough for a pile of books, magazines, plants, games, and her feet. She found this table in a thrift shop—it was a solid oak, four-foot square kitchen table. She says, "When the price dropped to $100 (principle #4),

I bought it, cut the legs off to the right height, and had my coffee table."

We also think creatively about how to do things for ourselves (principle #5). We spend a lot of time trying to solve problems. We ask for advice. We experiment. It is true that necessity is the mother of invention. We use our limited resources to find imaginative solutions for our decorating problems.

PRINCIPLE #4:
Learn to Be Patient and Content

The wonderful Christian attribute of patience is invaluable with regard to our decorating projects. Likewise is the Christian attribute of contentment. We are not perfect in these attributes, but the more we practice, the more skilled we become. While God is teaching us contentment and patience, our minds and feet are not idle. We continue to shop for the best deals, do research, and spread the word to our friends and family about our needs. We collect paint chips, write prices down in our little notebooks, and talk with our friends about what we want to do. We often change our minds about what it is we really need, so waiting time is not wasted.

Often we discover that we don't really want or need what we thought we did. Sometimes we discover a very inexpensive source for our needs. We received gifts because we let family and friends know what we needed. Recently, Jo's family received a wonderful solid oak coffee table from Jo's father. For several years, she had looked for a large coffee table with a shelf underneath. She rarely saw what she wanted, and never at an affordable price. She mentioned it to her father several times over the years. Finally, he said, "Give me the design and dimensions, and

I'll make it for you as a Christmas present." She did, and he did! Jo says, "It's far nicer than anything I imagined. There is no way we could afford a table of the quality and beauty we got."

By patiently waiting and repeatedly visiting the local thrift store, Gwen found four Queen Anne dining room chairs with the original leather seats. The seats were paint spattered and a little scuffed, but in surprisingly good condition. And they were navy blue, like a couple of wing back chairs she owned. Gwen rubbed the chair seats with a leather conditioning oil and had the chairs themselves refinished. Later a small solid maple sideboard showed up in a thrift shop. The top was badly scarred so Gwen had the refinisher sand it down. While he couldn't remove every vestige of the damage, only enough remained to give it character. Gwen's conclusion: "I not only had to be patient to find the furniture at a thrift store, I had to work hard to get it in good shape." Which brings us to our fifth point.

PRINCIPLE #5:
Do As Much As Possible Yourself

We have learned to become do-it-yourselfers. We will try just about anything. We get our hands filthy, break nails, and make big, lovely messes. And, yes, we also make mistakes, but we learn from them.

Gwen needed a sofa for her great room. She decided to slipcover one of her love seats. She had never made slipcovers before, and to this day doesn't know if she did it correctly. "I did it by trial and error, lots of fitting and resewing, and it looks great."

Jo had no idea what she was getting into when she decided to remove the ugly linoleum from her entryway so the wood floor could be seen. She just started pulling it up. The people who had laid the linoleum had used glue, nails, and duct tape to keep it down. Jo had to scrape, pull nails, fill holes, and sand and refinish the wood floor. It was hard, but she persevered. She had to redo the carpet edges that bordered the flooring. The nice guy at the hardware store provided helpful advice, so Jo figured out how to install flexible metal edging on the carpet.

The two of us have painted, wallpapered, patched, stained, fixed, and made things to save money. We are not experts—we had to read, ask questions, and do research. But the more we do, the more confident we become. We encourage you to have a can-do attitude. It gets things done.

PRINCIPLE #6:
Never Go in Debt When Decorating Your Home

The reason we have developed skills and become patient and creative is because we do not want to go into debt to do our projects. Although decorating is high on our priority list, staying within our budget is even more important. When you borrow money to decorate, you pay a lot more money than you think because of interest. So first, we tell our family about our ideas to get everyone's backing, then we budget, then we save. We wait patiently for items to go on sale or show up in a thrift store so we can more easily afford them. *We never pay full price for anything.*

Our desire to stay out of debt sometimes causes us to become *more* creative in problem solving. We have discovered there is no such thing as a once-in-a-lifetime deal, in spite of what ads and salespeople say. There will always be another sale, and if you're patient, you'll be amazed at what you can find at thrift stores and garage sales. Remember, a great deal is no longer a great deal if you have to borrow to get it.

When you stay out of debt and are patient, it's fun to see how your needs are met. One Christmas the Janssens gave each other a new pendant chandelier for their entryway. Unfortunately, the ceiling in that room is higher than any of their ladders can safely reach. Jo called around to electricians and discovered that it would cost about a hundred dollars to install it. They didn't pay that much for the fixture! So they waited. Six months later some friends came to visit. The father of the family is a tall electrician. By standing on the balcony, and with his very tall son's help, they were able to install the chandelier at no cost. Well, maybe not free—the whole family was well fed during their visit!

By now you've probably figured out that these six principles are intertwined. For example, avoiding debt requires patience. Coming up with creative solutions requires a do-it-yourself attitude. Buying quality items takes time and therefore patience. The waiting time will help you know exactly what you want. If you do your research you won't waste your money. You will know what your room should look like, what quality is, and where to find that item at the best price. That's what this book is all about.

It has taken us years to learn all of these skills. We have studied numerous decorating magazines and books in our quests to have beautiful homes. We pick up ideas everywhere we go, from home tours to hardware stores. Hopefully you will gain from our experience and avoid making the same mistakes.

To begin our process, we will examine a few major styles in order to help you decide what style best suits your home. That will become the foundation for developing your plan and implementing the ideas in this book.

CHAPTER 2

It's a Matter of Style

How do you like to live? Do you want to be surrounded by the latest technology, or is your goal to create a quiet haven away from the noise of the rest of the world? Do you prefer casual or formal rooms, or a little of both? Does your family thrive on sports? Music? Books? Entertaining? The answer to these questions and many more are important clues on how to decorate your home.

One time Gwen went with her brother to visit a woman who raised American foxhounds. (Now, a foxhound is not a cute little teacup-sized pup. These dogs, the kind you see chasing a fox in old prints, are rather large.) When Gwen and her brother walked into the kitchen, they saw numerous ribbons from dog shows posted everywhere around the room. There were leashes, dog dishes, sacks of dog food, and many other implements of dog care lying about. Right in the middle of this scene, standing on the table, was an American foxhound gobbling up leftovers from the family dinner. That house was about dogs and is an extreme example of one family's lifestyle.

Ted and Frances love to watch movies, so they have transformed their downstairs recreation room into a theater. With only one window, located on the north side of the house, this room is rather dark. The focal point is a large screen television, around which are grouped comfortable sofas and easy chairs. The walls are lined with shelves that hold hundreds of videos. This room fits their lifestyle.

Some families are more formal. Dan and Jan own a spacious home designed for entertaining in style. The furnishings include highly polished Queen Anne style tables and chairs. The windows are dressed with heavy, tasseled brocades. Crystal chandeliers hang from the ceiling. A social occasion in their home is always dressy. Jo has never seen either of them in sweats or jeans. They and their house are always ready for first-class entertaining.

Brenda's home is radically different from Jan and Dan's. When you come through the front door into an old-fashioned entryway, you find musical instruments, camera bags, and an easel or two. When you enter the living room, you realize you really are in a "living" room. There are musical instruments leaning against chairs and resting on their cushions. There is music stacked about, and a painting is resting on yet another easel. There is a comfortable disorder that reminds you of the stories about artists' garrets and the flats of musicians in New York City. It only takes a minute to conclude that this family loves the arts and the children are being trained in them.

Before you set a paintbrush to a wall or buy a piece of furniture, you need to determine *your* lifestyle. It's easy to get confused by the myriad of options and ideas you find in decorating magazines. The following will help you get oriented.

Research

By research, we're not suggesting the kind we hated doing for school papers. This should be fun. Begin at your local library. Leaf through their various decorating magazines, regardless of style. Look at *Country Living*, *Traditional Home*, *Metropolitan Home*, *Martha Stewart Living*, *Better Homes and Gardens*, *Architectural Digest*, and any others you can find. After leafing through them, you may decide that one or two styles catch your eye. They probably most reflect the style you want in your home.

Now it is time to invest a few dollars in decorating magazines that exemplify the look you like. This may mean an eclectic mix of country and traditional, or some other combination. If you don't feel your budget can handle this expense, call your local thrift stores and see if they carry old issues. You may be able to pick up a pile of magazines for very little.

As you look through the magazines, tear out or dog-ear the pages you really like. Jo prefers tearing out the pages so she can drop the clippings into files she has for each room in her house. Rather quickly you will discover that most of the pages you have selected have a few things in common. It may be a color, a style, or a feel. Keep a notebook where you will begin to record all of your notes, decorating ideas, and insights from your research.

Jo has two notebooks so she won't forget any details or ideas for decorating her home. She keeps a small, spiral-bound pad in her purse, and another three-ring binder—it sits on her desk and is part of her schedule book—to record her needs, ideas, plans, and any details about her projects. Divide your notebook into sections, one for each room. We'll refer to this notebook again later.

Another part of research is visiting furniture stores in your area to see which ones you like best. Some, such as Ethan Allen, specialize in traditional furnishings and have just one category of furniture. Others, particularly chain stores like J.C. Penney's, have a smorgasbord of styles. Discover which stores best reflect your likes.

Another source of ideas is catalogs. Spiegel, J. C. Penney, Bombay Company, and Ethan Allen all have nice catalogs. Many local furniture stores also produce catalogs. Go through them, tear out pictures of those items you like, and drop them into a file folder for future reference.

Basic Styles

Another helpful exercise is to go through your home with your new decorating notebook and take inventory of your stuff. We're going to describe a few basic styles. Write down what items you have in each particular style. For example, go into your living room and list all things that are clearly traditional—

perhaps your lamps and window coverings fall into that category. Next, list the elements that fit best in the country category, and so on. Some things could fit in more than one style—write them down in *each* category.

Most of us have an eclectic mix of stuff. However, you may discover that your favorite things belong to a particular style. Go through every room in your house and finish your recording. Don't forget to record things hidden away in boxes and cupboards. This exercise will give you an idea of what style you are most attracted to. It will also show you what you have to work with as you decide which direction to take.

Now let's look at four basic styles.

Traditional

This style depends on old things and antiques, but it can take on many looks, such as Classical Greek, European, French, Italian, English, American, or a combination of all the above. The details of traditional design include anything old, such as the leather and oak of a men's-only club, moldings on walls or ornate ceilings, neat, symmetrical room arrangements of old curvy furniture, built-in bookshelves, screens, paneled doors, a grand piano, marble or iron garden furniture, and heavy, layered, rich-colored window treatments. Floors are real wood, topped with patterned carpet or needlepoint or Oriental rugs. Walls may have an aged look created by paint treatments, historic wallpapers, and decorative textures created with paint techniques, such as marbling, ragging, or sponging. Preferred fabrics tend to be leather, silk, satin, damask, brocade, fur throws, and other rich fabrics with fringe and tassel trims.

It is the accessories that add up to the heirloom quality of a traditional room. They may include items made with crystal, silver, gold leaf, polished wood, and polished marble. You might want to include flowers, travel mementos, a candelabra, a bowl of fruit, a Chinese bowl, a silver tea service on a silver tray, candlesticks, or old-looking china. Artwork will be framed ornately in silver, gold leaf, or heavy wood. The art itself, usually done in oils, will include landscapes, hunting scenes, still lifes, botanical prints, and old portraits.

There are variations on the traditional style, such as Victorian—lots of things on display, dark colors, lots of patterns and velvets—or opulent European, where you pretend you're in an English castle or a French mansion. These rooms have lots of gilt and rich fabric with fringes. There's the world traveler look—a neutral background for all the fine antiques and collectibles brought from your world travels. Or Classical Greek—pillars of marble and granite, the Greek key and other simple motifs, marble statuary, and old garden furniture. Colors tend to be black, brown, and tan. Finally there is the Gothic look—high arches, marble, stained glass, deep colors, and dark woods.

You can choose from any period and country for a pure look of one style, or you can combine several. (See illustration 2.1.)

Contemporary

This style depends on sleek surfaces, hand-crafted wood, marble, chrome, glass, and textural variety. There is an uncomplicated look of sophistication, clean lines, neutral colors and bright pastels, a lack of clutter, and use of built-in furniture. Upholstery, rugs, and window fabrics are of natural textures: leather, suede, raw silk, linen, wool, and nubby, woven fabric. Floors that aren't carpeted will be of wood, slate, or marble. Windows are unadorned so the view can be appreciated, or they are dressed simply with miniblinds, Roman blinds, vertical blinds, or pleated shades. Track or recessed lighting and

Illustration 2.1
Traditional grouping

Illustration 2.2
Contemporary grouping

torchères enhance these rooms. Art will be big, bold, and modern with simple frames or no frames at all, or black-and-white photographs in simple frames with large matting. (See illustration 2.2.)

Country

There are various country styles, including English, Americana, Southwestern, European, Scandinavian, and Colonial. Country style is a less formal look that uses folk art and rustic furniture as well as antiques. The antiques, or reproductions of antiques, will include farm tools, toys, weather vanes, kitchenware, baskets, jars, quilts, folk art, garden tools, and birdhouses. Furnishings may include painted furniture; hand-crafted chairs; primitive pieces; twig and wicker furniture, or stuffed sofas and chairs covered in chintz, homespun textiles, calico, ticking, plaids, or gingham. Floors may be wood, brick, or flagstones, and covered with hooked rugs, rag rugs, stenciled floor cloths, or dhurries. Details include items made of pine, tin, iron, or painted wood, and are drawn from the farm, country, or pioneer days. Ceilings may consist of exposed beams. Walls can be done in pine paneling, brick walls, simple stenciled designs on white walls, and pretty country floral wallpapers.

Variations on the country style include English country—a combination of checks, stripes, simple plaids, and small geometrics in various scales, along with lots of primary or pastel colors combined with white ruffles and country-style antiques. Another is the cottage style. This has a particularly cozy, summery feel, with lots of white, painted furniture, wicker, and other outside items brought inside, such as flowers and gardening accessories. There is an ethnic country style using textiles, folk art, and anything culturally significant from a particular ethnic group. There is Santa Fe country that uses Indian blankets, cowboy paraphernalia, western art, leather, rough-hewn wood, stones, rustic furnishings, cacti, and desert colors. Finally, there's Scandinavian country that emphasizes simplicity and uses pastels (especially blue) and white or off-white colors, painted furniture, bare windows, and no clutter. As with traditional, a country look can be based on any culture, region, or era. (See illustration 2.3.)

Eclectic

Very few of us have homes that are purely one style or another—most homes are eclectic, which is a combination of elements from various styles. This scheme can be more of a challenge to pull together. There needs to be unifying ambience, colors, and theme. For example, a country style family room may include a modern floor lamp with a finish, material, or color that is repeated somewhere else in the room. Country and traditional styles are the easiest to combine because so many of their elements, such as antiques, can go either way.

Jo has an Egyptian rug in her living room that gives the country wicker coffee table a more traditional feel. Or is it the other way around? The clean lines of a contemporary glass coffee table in a traditional room can add shine and sophistication.

Scale becomes very important when combining different styles. If things have the same scale or bulk and look like they feel comfortable with each other, then they can safely be put together in the same room. However, it is tricky. Ask someone you trust if things go together. Study decorating magazines to see successful ways to combine different styles.

Since the eclectic style is so personal and can take on so many variations, we will stick to discussing the first three styles in the following chapters. (See illustration 2.4.)

Illustration 2.3
Country grouping

Illustration 2.4
Eclectic grouping

Ambience

Besides the style of your room, you must also consider the ambience. By this we mean the feel, mood, and personality of a room. There are four basic types of ambience. Although a room can have more than one ambience, a single mood will usually prevail. Sometimes you can alter a room's mood for a special occasion. Read through the following descriptions and you will see that certain ambience may apply best to certain rooms. For instance, formal may be most appropriate for a living room or dining room, but not children's bedrooms. Those may be better suited to a fun mood.

Formal

A formal room is not one where you generally put up your feet or play with the dog. Our public living areas and master bedrooms often have a formal feel. Some folks may find such impressive showplaces intimidating, but others feel right at home in them. Formal rooms are the places to use fine fabrics that will not be exposed to much wear or frequent spills and dirt. You might use silk, chintz, linen, velvet, brocade, damask, and other shiny fabrics; leather can be very formal also. Surfaces are well cared for and polished. Shiny things like crystal, glass, brass, gold, chrome, and porcelain signify the formal ambience. Art is serious and well framed. Furnishings, art, and accessories are often arranged symmetrically. A formal room may have a "museum" or "be-on-your-best-behavior" feel to them.

Casual

Casual ambience is a more laid-back feel. Rooms are welcoming and comfortable and not at all intimidating. You can put your feet on the coffee table or tuck them under you on the chair. Many homes are casual throughout, especially in the West. With our busy lifestyles and informal entertaining, a casual room makes a lot of sense. Often the presence of children and pets dictates a more casual ambience.

In a casual ambience, surfaces should not require a great deal of care and worry, but instead are sturdy and can take heavy wear. Fabrics are durable, can withstand a few spills, and will hide stains. They include plaids, floral prints, sturdy cottons, denim, sailcloth, corduroy, and synthetics that look and feel comfortable on the skin. The textures are not as refined, smooth, or shiny as in formal rooms—they can be nubby, rough, or distressed.

Fun

This is a lighthearted place that says, "We have a sense of humor, so play and have fun!" Often this is the ambience desired for a playroom, recreation room, or kids' bedrooms, although we have seen entire homes decorated in this playful mood. You can accomplish a sense of fun through color and motif. If you have kids, there will probably be at least one room in your home that has a fun ambience. Some of you have personalities that are fun, carefree, and lighthearted. Feel free to express fun somewhere in your home.

It is hard to take these rooms too seriously. Surfaces are very durable: well-protected wood, melamine laminates (durable plastic surface laminated to particle board), plastic, vinyls, smooth floors—anything that withstands spills and hard wear. Colors are bright or primary. Designs are bold, fun, simple, even humorous. For walls, a simple coat of semigloss paint, scrubbable wallpaper, or even large-scale renditions of comic book characters painted on the wall are appropriate. Like hard surfaces, fabrics also need to withstand hard wear and spills;

these include denim, sailcloth, corduroy, leather, and vinyl. Art could include simply framed posters in playful, bold designs.

Romantic

While a romantic look might be desired for a whole house, it is usually reserved for a bedroom, dining room, or living room. This mood is restful, comfortable, soft, and romantic. It helps to create a place where you feel like putting your mind in neutral, relaxing with someone you love, reading a good book, enjoying soft music, and basically unwinding. Such rooms are usually used by adults.

Romantic rooms use a lot of white and pastels, often with a monochromatic color scheme. Typically, there is a generous amount of fabrics on beds, windows, and tables, and plenty of lace, flowers, plants, candles, and pillows. Soft lighting from lamps is preferred to harsh, overhead lighting. The look inspires not only romance, but also comfort and ease.

Your Decorating Notebook

As you do your research and homework, you are going to come up with many ideas. That's why we recommend you start your personal decorating notebook as a place to record observations, ideas, colors, and so on. In each part you can tape, clip, staple, or glue paint chips, swatches of fabric, wallpaper samples, and pieces of carpeting. Record your plans and needs for each room. Include dimensions of the things you need. For example, if you need a rug, write down its approximate dimensions. You may want a desk but you only have thirty-three inches of space to put it in. Better write that down. Write down window measurements if you plan to redo the window treatments. Keep this information with you when you shop. (And keep a small measuring tape in your purse as well—it's invaluable.)

When you shop, record the place, price, and description of things you've found so that when you have the money, you won't forget where you saw that great little item.

Jo includes a section in her notebook for the projects she wants to do. These are divided into big-ticket items that cost a lot of money and cheap or no-cost projects and items. She puts approximate dollar amounts next to big-ticket items, so she can know what she is aiming for in her budget. Next to her no-cost items she notes if it has to be done in the summer. She spends long, cold winter days wishing she could paint a room, collecting paint chips, and waiting for warm weather to do the job.

Your notebook will also help you plan projects. Not only can you record prices, but you can list all the things you need to complete a project. As you do research, the list will become longer and more specific. You can record bids, estimates, addresses of out-of-the-way resources, and so much more—all in one place so you don't lose all that information by trying to keep many little slips of paper.

Your notebook needs to be small enough to keep in your purse so you don't leave home without it. If this seems too much, at least keep a pared down notebook with the essential shopping information and have the more detailed notebook at home as Jo does. You never know when someone is going to tell you about just the place to find that one-of-a-kind lamp at a price you can afford.

Now We Know

To redecorate a room or your entire home, you will need to thoroughly think about each room's function, style, and any themes or motifs you want in it. We have provided a questionnaire in appendix A to help you and your family evaluate your needs. For public rooms, work through the whole questionnaire. For personal rooms, such as bedrooms, begin with the "Color" section. The questionnaire should be completed separately for each room. Write down any conclusions in your notebook. This can be filled out all at once, or before your next project.

By the time you've worked through this process, you will have a pretty good idea what your family needs for living space, comfort level, work space, and lifestyle.

Congratulations! Many people never get this far. They've never really thought about what makes a home a special place, or why some homes are comfortable and some make the occupants restless and eager to get away.

In the next chapter, we'll start looking at how to pull all this information together and develop a decorating plan that will fit your lifestyle, your pocketbook, and your family's need for beauty, comfort, and security.

Shoestring Tips

- Look for back issues of decorating magazines at thrift stores.
- Look for decorating and how-to books at used bookstores. But before you buy, check the publishing date of the book to make sure it's recent enough to be useful.
- Check out decorating books at the library.
- Visit model homes, open houses, and the "Parade of Homes" or "Street of Dreams" (where local builders show fully decorated homes) for current decorating trends.
- When you see something you don't like, always ask yourself why. Learning what not to do is just as valuable as learning what to do.
- Get organized with a decorating notebook and files to capture ideas.

CHAPTER 3

What's the Big Idea?

Jo's friend, Cindy, was excited about her purchase of a Victorian home with "lots of potential." On moving day she gave Jo a tour. The previous owners had done a lot of "updating." From the grand entry hall Jo and Cindy could see straight ahead into the family room and beyond it into the kitchen. To their right was the front parlor and through it they could see the dining room. To their left were the front stairs. Every room they saw had a different color of carpeting, 70s' style wall and window treatments. It was a horrible hodgepodge of tasteless decor.

But Cindy had two things going for her: she had a plan to restore the home to its original beauty, and she is married to a wonderful handyman, Mike, who was willing to do a lot of work. With hope reigning, shortly after moving day, Mike and Cindy began tearing into the house, one room at a time. We'll tell you about the miraculous transformation of this house as we go along.

If you have read the previous chapter and filled out the questionnaire in the appendix, you should now have some idea of the style and ambience you want for your home. One word of caution: Make sure you consider the personality and style of your husband and children. After all, it is their home too. So the more you include them in your plans, the more supportive they will be—and of course, the more enthusiastically they will help you!

After you've agreed with your family on some basic ideas about how you want your home to look, it's time to start working on the common living areas—those areas that the family shares and the guests see. Having a master plan—or at least a master idea—helps you take advantage of sales, thrift store finds, and other opportunities to save money on furnishings for these areas.

What Atmosphere Am I Trying to Create in My Home?

Most of us want to create a safe, quiet place where our families can escape from the stress of jobs, school, shopping malls, and too many people. One way to achieve this peaceful atmosphere is to give the common living areas of your home a unified look and feel. To accomplish this goal, all the common areas need to follow either the same or complementary themes. This means similar colors, similar fabrics, and a similar theme. Suppose you were walking through a home where one room was done in green, the next in a shocking orange, and the third in a rose color. That home would feel disruptive, chaotic, confusing—anything but restful. Or suppose the living room is done in black and white with chrome furniture and marble tabletops, and the family room is done all in ruffles and wood tones. Walking through such a house would be like walking through display rooms at a local furniture store. It would jar your senses, to say the least.

A unified color scheme and overall decorating style is more restful, more pleasing to the senses, and can even be more economical than a jumble of styles and color. By using the same paint color, or shades of that same color, and the same flooring throughout, you will be able to move furniture from one room to another, and it will look as though those furniture pieces were purchased for that exact spot. Cindy chose the Victorian style for her home. She started her redecorating by tearing up the carpets and going with natural wood floors and deep greens and reds to unify the living spaces on the first floor.

If you like an eclectic style, rather than filling one room with modern furniture and the next with antiques, find a way to mix them in the same room. Gwen saw this done very successfully in a home where the couple used Oriental rugs and large pieces of antique European furniture mixed with glass, chrome, and leather. Each room was anchored with an Oriental rug and a few pieces of antique leather and modern leather furniture. Some accessories were antiques; others were modern. Many modern pieces have curvy lines that meld well with the fluid lines of antiques.

Color As Part of the Big Idea

Your first challenge when decorating is to decide on an overall color scheme, theme, and style for the common areas of your home. Begin by painting all the walls the same color or subtle shades of the same color. For example, you might use tones in the tan, brown, and cream family of colors. All through the living area, walls could be painted a creamy off-white. The kitchen might have a matching cream-colored, satin-finished paint for easy cleaning. Or you could use a wallpaper wainscoting in a subtle design in a similar beige or cream-colored background. For fun, the main floor powder room could be done in a wild floral wallpaper with a cream-colored background. Or you could paper it in a cream-colored moiré pattern.

In the adjoining dining room, you could sponge a beige texture over the cream background. Add a lovely border of leaves and fruits in neutral tones stenciled near the ceiling. Just think how charming such a dining room would be when the table is covered with a brown tablecloth, off-white dishes, napkins with an all-over leaf print, and cream-colored candles in brass holders on either side of a large bowl of fruit.

As mentioned earlier, Gwen uses the basic colors of red and blue against a neutral background in all of her rooms. Any fabrics she chooses are in those basic colors. For example, she has a chair and matching hassock upholstered in a fabric with a cream background and a blue and red floral pattern. Those two pieces have been moved from bedroom to living room to family room, and now own a spot on an upstairs landing where Gwen has created a reading corner.

Do you get the idea? All rooms that are visible from another room should have a similar color hue. To further enhance this idea, use the same flooring material throughout the common area. In our beige and brown color scheme you might choose a tan carpeting, or if you are brave, a creamy-white tone. In the kitchen you would probably want an easy-care surface like tile, vinyl flooring, or wood. You might want to have wood floors throughout the common areas. No matter what kind of flooring you choose for the kitchen, its tone and shade of color should be similar to the floors that butt up against it. If you have tan carpeting all the way through the house, choose a kitchen flooring with a similar color tone. Cindy removed barn siding and cedar shingles from her walls and has coordinated red and green wallpaper throughout the first floor. Her wood floors have coordinated area rugs. Red and green upholstered Victorian furnishings are in every room. What was once a hodgepodge is now beautifully coordinated from the front door to the back.

Choose Fabrics That Lend Themselves to the Overall Scheme

The next consideration is the fabrics you will use. Because draperies, curtains, and upholstered pieces are large surfaces, they make a big impact in a room. All fabrics used in the public areas need to coordinate. Would anyone enjoy a room that had a country print sofa flanked by a pair of chairs upholstered in

tropical prints? We know—just the thought of it is awful! We exaggerate to make the point.

The safest color choices for longevity are neutrals or solids. Choose a color your family likes very much and can live with for a long time. If you want to mix and match, visit a fabric store where you can see delightful displays of coordinating fabrics. Fabrics that are designed to go together will include solids in one to three colors, a print or two, and usually stripes or checks. If you find a designer fabric group you like, use one fabric for the kitchen windows, the same fabric design in a larger scale in the dining room, and stripes and/or checks in an adjoining family room. Cover the sofa in one of the solid colors of the fabric group, and fill it with throw pillows made from the dining room and kitchen fabrics. You'll be considered a decorating genius!

If you decide to use a checked fabric, vary the sizes of the checks. This adds variety to the room, but maintains a unified look through the use of a single color.

Window Treatments

Jo and Gwen handle window treatments differently, but the principles of using the basic colors remain the same. Jo uses off-white treatments in all the public spaces. She has hung off-white valances as close to the ceiling as possible over the top of the windows throughout the common areas of her home. This fools the eye into thinking the window is larger than it is. Under the valances she uses honeycomb pleated fabric shades for both warmth and protection from the sun. Gwen uses toppers: blue-and-white checked in the family room and kitchen and blue-and-burgundy-striped swags and tails lined with dusty pink in the more formal living-dining room area.

Upholstery

Sofas and chairs are big visually—they are usually what you see first when you come into a room. They are also the most expensive part of your decorating budget, and as "shoestring decorators," we will not be replacing upholstery very often. We must take care in choosing upholstery and slipcover fabrics. Obviously these fabrics need to coordinate with your overall color scheme and with window coverings, wall colors, and flooring.

Cindy's front parlor has a sofa and love seat done in a lovely tapestry-like floral in greens and reds. With five sons, she needs upholstery that hides dirt well!

Here are some tips on fabric selection:
- Darker shades will make a room cozy.
- White and very light colors brighten a room.
- Light fabric colors make a room seem larger.
- Light fabrics show dirt and stains easily.
- Busy fabric prints will hide dirt and stains.
- Busy fabric prints add interest and excitement to a room.
- Big patterns require big rooms.
- Solids are easier to coordinate with accessories, themes, and motifs.
- Stripes and checks coordinate nicely with prints and solids.
- Orlon, nylon, and some other synthetics as well as wool and wool blends are generally durable. (Furniture and fabric store personnel can help you choose fabrics to meet your durability needs.)
- Some fabrics are soil resistant.
- Smooth textures look formal; rough ones are more casual.
- Different textures in the room give variety and interest.
- Some nubby-textured fabrics can catch on things, so take care in choosing these fabrics.
- Highly textured fabrics hide dirt better.
- Chintzes, cottons, and linens show soil and wear sooner.
- Furniture fabric should be comfortable to bare skin.
- Drapery and other window fabrics should be lined to look more finished and to protect them from sun damage.

If you are redoing an entire room, it helps to create a sample board to see how all the elements will work together. Purchase a big piece of poster board at least two by three feet. Assemble on the board swatches and paint chips for the colors you plan to use in the room.

> *A tip for pulling it all together*

Go to a paint store and get the largest paint chip you can find. In some cases these might be as big as two by three inches. At some point, you might want to buy a pint of the wall paint you are considering and paint the entire posterboard so you can truly get a feel for how the color will work with your other swatches. If you plan to use wallpaper or wallpaper borders, get the biggest samples the store will let you have. In some cases, your sample might be in a wallpaper book. Check it out and take it home. You won't be able to detach the page from the book, but by propping the book open, you can get a pretty good feel for how things will look together.

Go to the carpet store and get big pieces of carpet. If you are planning new upholstery, get big swatches. If you can afford it, buy a yard of the fabric. A little invested in samples now can prevent your getting a whole room full of carpet, paint, fabrics, or wallpaper and then saying, "This isn't what I wanted. I never envisioned it looking like this!"

Put the swatches onto the board in about the same proportions that they will be in your room. This means a *big* piece of carpeting, a *big* paint chip, a *smaller* swatch of drapery or upholstery fabric. Put a photo of a lamp or other accessory items on the board as well. Just a word here: There's nothing to say you can't go to a lamp or furniture store and take pictures of the items you *hope* to purchase. Also, the store may have full-color brochures of the items you want. Merchants can be amazingly helpful when they think they have a live customer on the hook.

When your decorating board is ready, put it in the room and live with it for a while. Move the display to different places in the room to see how light affects the colors. If your selections seem to work together, you might consider purchasing larger samples and going through the same process you did with the smaller display panel.

If you are only buying new carpeting, get the largest sample the supplier has and bring it home for a week or two. If upholstery or curtains are what you're replacing, get samples to bring home. If an upholstery shop or fabric store doesn't have samples, buy a yard or two of your chosen fabric and try it out in your home. The sample can always be used later for throw pillows. Drape it over a sofa or hang it at the window and once again live with it for a while. When you walk into the room after being out for a while, how do these fabrics, colors, and textures affect you? Are you pleased? Is the effect not quite right? If not, can you identify why? Now you know what to try next.

If, for some reason, you can't bring samples home, then take samples to the store. Spread out fabrics, paint samples, sofa cushions, and so on at the store. Store personnel have always been helpful when we've done this. We look like intelligent, serious customers. But if they are annoyed, just remember that this is a major expenditure for you and sales for them. This is something you need to do so that you don't waste your decorating dollars. It's your money, so spend it wisely, and do what you need to do to make sure you are making the right decisions.

Following this advice will avoid the problem a friend encountered when he chose a piece of fabric at the upholstery shop. He thought it was a perfect match for the blue carpeting in his home, so he told the upholstery people to go ahead with recovering the chair. A few weeks later, it was delivered to his home, and, to his horror, he discovered the chair was a blue-green and the carpet was a blue-gray. The clash was awful!

Our minds cannot accurately remember colors. There are too many variations, shades, tones, and hues. We also need to remember that the lighting conditions in a shop are not the same as in our homes. Therefore, the colors will not appear as they do at home. That's why it's vital to take samples home. *Never try to match color from memory.*

Choose Solids

Durable solids of top quality materials are always a good choice for upholstery fabrics. Most of us tend to tire of prints after a while. Then we either have to live with the pattern or print or spend a lot of money to recover furniture that may not need new upholstery. We both love decorating with solid-colored fabrics because they never go out of style. They also can be moved from one setting to another. We use patterns and prints in throw pillows, tablecloths, and accessories.

Jo's first experiences with sofa-buying convinced her of the need to buy solid-colored fabrics. Her first sofa was an inexpensive (this experience also taught Jo to buy quality) floral-print design. After a few years—very few—the sofa sagged and her family was sick of the print. So she bought a high quality sofa upholstered in a big plaid, in shades of blue and beige on a white background. Plaids were all the rage at the time, and Jo was happy to have found one in her decorating colors. Seven years later her family was once again tired of the plaid, but guess what? Because of the great quality, the upholstery was still in good condition. She solved the problem by selling the sofa and buying a light blue, solid-colored sofa. Nine years later they are still enjoying it, and it still fits with their lifestyle and decorating plan, even though the Janssens have moved a couple of times since buying it. To redecorate Jo simply changes the throw pillows, replaces a small area rug, and adds a new afghan for a color accent.

Reupholster or Slipcover?

Gwen has had the same sofa for years. A friend, who was an interior designer, recommended she purchase a sofa of good quality. That sofa is on its third covering and is still one of the most comfortable pieces of furniture in the house. Jo's sister has had the same sofa for many years. She taught herself to upholster furniture and has recovered the sofa four times. That's a *great* way to save money!

If you can't afford new upholstery and can't find or make slipcovers, there is another way. There is a trend toward covering sofas with large pieces of fabric strategically tied in place. You can find instructions in many pattern books.

When Gwen moved from Colorado to Michigan, the sofa that has been recovered three times didn't look right in her new family room. So she bought two inexpensive quilts from a close-out bin at a fabric store and used the above technique for a quick and inexpensive cover job for the sofa. Since the quilts whip off easily, she can shake them outside to get rid of pet hair, or she can wash them, fluff them up, and put them back. The quilts also keep the sofa clean and are very comfortable to the skin—even during sticky Michigan summers.

Now the Fun Begins!

Understanding whether your family is formal or casual or a combination of both is important in developing a big-picture plan for your decorating. A master plan, or at least a master idea, makes it possible to take advantage of sales, thrift store finds, and other shoestring decorating opportunities. When you see a remarkable bargain, you'll know instantly whether or not that item will fit into your home's theme. Once you have decided the basics—color, comfort, and style—you can begin to accumulate accessory items to give your home a very special feeling and character.

If your family is the formal type and a brass chandelier presents itself at a resale shop, you'll know it is perfect to hang over your Duncan Phyfe dining room table. If your family is casual and you find some wonderful wicker chairs at a garage sale, you'll know in an instant they've been waiting for you.

Picking a Theme

Both of us find it easier to decorate a house or a room if it has a theme. Once you've picked a theme, you find more things that "fit" than you would ever have imagined. Friends, too, make contributions to your theme room and seem pleased to be able to give you something lasting for your home.

Gwen's last four houses have had a "Dutch" family room-kitchen combination. It began quite by chance when she discovered some hand-painted delft tiles from Holland in a house she was having remodeled. "Be sure those tiles don't walk away," she told the contractor. "I have plans for them." There were only a few delft tiles so she mixed them with cobalt blue tiles and set them together in a fireplace surround. Then she hung a photo enlargement of five Dutch windmills taken at Kinderdyke, Holland, over the fireplace.

In her next house, she wanted to use the same idea again, but had no tiles. Although it was an unlikely place, she found delft tiles in a restaurant that serves Dutch food. She bought several—they are quite expensive—and once again mixed them with cobalt blue tiles for the family room fireplace surround.

Then she began to find *many* objects for her Dutch room. She purchased several pieces of delftware from thrift shops and found European ring lace valances with woven windmills. Ring lace is expensive, but she has used it again and again. It will probably be handed down to her children, as it is extremely durable. Friends gave her even more delft pieces. She framed a print of work done by the Dutch painter Vermeer. A friend gave her a copper coal scoop with a delft handle. Her daughter gave her a pair of old-fashioned skates found in a flea market in Holland. She is using all the same pieces in a fourth house and still receives rave reviews, but more importantly, she is still enjoying the blue-and-white Dutch decor. Her accent color continues to be colonial red.

Jo's theme is gardening. In details all through her home, you will find flowers, pictures of flowers and gardens, birdhouses, butterflies, and birds. She uses them in art, borders, fabrics, wallpaper, pillows, accessories, lamps, lamp shades, curtain tiebacks, rugs, collections, coasters, tablecloths, pictures books, trays, vases, and more.

Her powder room is a lot of fun and inevitably draws comments from her guests. She painted a garden scene on all the walls, beginning with a picket fence, a vine crawling up a trellis, birds, butterflies, a birdhouse, and even a rake painted to look as if it is leaning in the corner. A birdhouse rests on the back of the toilet tank, and decorative towels have birds embroidered on them. The lotion and soap dispensers have a floral design. This tiny room is even more fun when you close the door and find a sign painted on the door that has been positioned around the doorknob. It reads "Occupied." Above it is a crescent moon reminiscent of an old-fashioned outhouse. By the way, you don't have to be a great artist to do this type of thing. Jo did most of it with stencils.

Private Rooms vs. Public

So far we have only talked about the public rooms. Let's talk now about the rooms that are not usually seen by guests. These can have a completely different style and scheme from the public rooms. (Gwen doesn't even know how a Dutch bedroom would look.) You will want to keep the flooring the same throughout the house for continuity.

Bedrooms, offices, bathrooms, and other hidden-away rooms will reflect the tastes of individuals who use them more than the public rooms will. Later in the book we will give you lots of ideas for making those rooms fit individual personalities. You need to use the questionnaire in appendix A for each room, beginning with the part about choosing colors. The colors you choose for these rooms need to go with the flooring. Plan to make a separate color board for each room.

When someone opens the front door to your home and walks into the common living areas, that person should feel there is continuity from one room to the next and that you have thought through your decorating plan. Visitors should be able quickly to learn something about the tastes, activities, and interests of the people who live in this house.

When you go into the Janssen's house, you know immediately that these are book people. An entire wall of built-in bookcases full of books is visible from the entry. You'll also pick up on Jo's gardening theme as soon as you spot those two topiary trees painted on the wall facing the front door and see the ivy twined through the chandelier over the dining room table.

When you come into Gwen's home, you'll know even before you enter that she has a hunt theme inside, because on the front porch is a low bench painted in a colonial blue-green color that matches the trim of the interior décor. Beside the bench is a pair of riding boots. Hanging from a wooden peg above the bench are a black velvet riding helmet and a horse bridle. An English hunt horn adorns the door itself is. Thus her theme is introduced before you even enter the house.

You have probably figured out by now that this decorating thing will take some time and effort. You're right! But anything worth doing is worth doing right. The planning, shopping, thinking, and research will pay off in a beautiful home, and it *can* be done on a shoestring.

A lot of the fun of shoestring decorating is shopping for all the things you need to pull a room together. In the next chapter we will tell you about our favorite places that help us stay within our budget.

CHAPTER 4

Shopping on a Shoestring

$\mathcal{Y}$ ou've decided on colors, themes, style, and ambiance. You have a vague idea of how you want your rooms to look someday. Now it's time to open your eyes, your ears, your mind, *and* your mouth. Start watching for sales, including yard sales. Check the paper for used goods. Ask friends where to get good deals on the items you need. Let your friends and family know what you want so they can keep their eyes and ears open for solutions. They may even donate things you need or give them to you on gift-giving occasions. Go through the classified ads in the phone book. Outlets, closeout places, and factories often have great deals.

Al and Jo needed a sofa and happened to mention it to friends. Their friends told them about a furniture store in the country that sells brand-name furniture slightly above cost. It seems a farmer had converted his barn into a very simple and unattractive showroom. He spent no money on advertising and didn't have to pay rent for expensive mall space. What he saved on marketing and overhead he passed along to his customers,

and, as a result, word spread. When Jo arrived at the "barn" she was ready. She had done her homework and knew just the brand, style, and upholstery she wanted. Of course, the owner did not have that model on the floor, but he was willing to order it. Even with the special order, the cost was probably half of what it would have been at a glitzy, uptown furniture store.

If you don't know where a "barn" that sells furniture is located, and you have to go to a regular furniture store, be advised that most of them have a closeout area in the back of the store. Often the pieces found in this room are damaged, but sometimes overstocked items or last year's models are also available. One of the large department store chains in Seattle has a closeout store that sells appliances, electronics, sofas, beds, and all other kinds of household furnishings. Once Gwen bought a mattress without the box springs. She already had box springs that were adequate, but it's almost impossible to buy one without the other. For some reason the closeout store had the very mattress she wanted, and there were no matching box springs. For about $100 she was set up for comfortable sleeping.

You may be thinking our examples don't fit you. No one's made or given you a nice piece of furniture. You've never found a perfect, out-of-the-way place with inexpensive yet quality furniture. Our encouragement to you is this: You never know *how* your needs may be met. Gwen once heard about a man who lived in New York City who picked up a complete set of original Hitchcock chairs in front of an apartment building on trash day. You don't know what you might find or what might be given to you. Be receptive to new ideas and broaden the possibility-factor. America is an affluent country, and that affluence is creating a virtual flood of used goods. People think they want something. They buy it, then decide they really didn't want it. They sell it for a song or give it away, and there it is, just waiting for you.

No doubt, there's a place in your community that's a unique source of inexpensive items. Jo lives in a town with a lot of military personnel. They are frequently transferred overseas, and moving their stuff is expensive. Consequently, one can pick up large, heavy items like refrigerators, washers, and dryers at remarkable prices. Jo bought an excellent treadmill at a fraction of the normal price.

In Gwen's town, the Kiwanis Club has a garage sale for three hours every Saturday morning. People donate items from Drexel dining room sets to fur coats and everything in between. Kiwanis volunteers sort, price, and display all of this stuff. Volunteers also run the sale, and buyers come by the hundreds. Gwen overheard one of the volunteers say that they had taken in about $4,000 during one three-hour stint. The proceeds are used for charity purposes. Everybody wins—including you! If

Gwen is looking for something, she usually looks there first. Just recently she bought a solid brass bed for thirty-five dollars. Not bad!

Many of the following options are available where you live: thrift stores, resale shops, bartering or trading, garage or yard sales, outlet stores, and more.

Thrift Stores

One of Jo's favorite pastimes is thrift store shopping. Jo and her friend Vickie make regular visits to their favorite stores, including Goodwill and Salvation Army stores. The trips are planned, so they know exactly where they're going and don't backtrack. They have their lists, complete with measurements, and share them with each other so each can help look for the other's wants. They pack water bottles and snacks, and take turns preparing lunches for the two of them. There's always the temptation to stop at a restaurant for lunch, but they're both living on a shoestring, and eating out would only stretch it closer to the breaking point.

Shopping with a friend is a great idea. Jo and Vickie are very honest with each other as they evaluate possible purchases. Often one will see a fatal flaw in an item that the other missed. The temptations to spend too much are lessened because of where they shop. Many times they come home empty-handed, but never empty-hearted—they always have fun. And when they do make a purchase, it helps to know that in many cases they are helping out a worthy charity.

As Jo looks around her home, she sees numerous items she's purchased at thrift stores, including dressers, headboards, a desk, a table, clothes, sheets, dishes, silverware, a piano bench, and a lamp. Both of us have found great quality furniture of all kinds and styles.

Of course, if you have a particular need and you're shopping at thrift stores, you must be patient. We recommend visiting the stores once a week if you can, because new items arrive all the time. Some stores will take your name and a description of the item you want and call you if it comes in. Also, ask about shipment days—what days certain items are put on the floor. If the shop puts out furniture on Thursdays, you'll want to get there Thursday morning—the quality items often go fast.

Not everything in these stores is of the best quality. You need to inspect items carefully. By browsing in quality furniture stores, your eye will learn to recognize quality. Don't be afraid to look behind items and turn them upside down or inside out. Avoid items made with particle board or plywood. Real wood and good veneers are best. Check drawers: joints that are just glued or screwed together are not as good as tongue and groove, dovetail, double dowel, or mortise and tenon joints. The back panel of fine furniture is finished and inset and screwed on the frame. Upholstered furniture, where the legs and frame meet, should have a corner block glued and screwed—not nailed or stapled. Coils should be hand-tied, and the webbing underneath should be closely spaced together. Springs that have sprung can be retied, but get a book on upholstery to find out how to reach it and do it right.

Look carefully to see if an item needs minor repairs, refinishing, reupholstering, or a slipcover. Know what you can and cannot fix and do. A chair should not wobble. A wooden chair may simply need to be reglued and rescrewed. To do that, unscrew the block under the seat, scrape off the old glue, reapply new glue, and rescrew. If the hole for a screw is too big, insert toothpicks or wooden matches.

If the legs and stretchers are the problem, carefully take them apart, sand off any old glue, and make the joining parts a little fatter by gluing on a few rounds of thin thread. After that dries, glue the chair back together, being careful not to get glue where you will want stain, because you cannot stain over glue. Wrap the chair legs with rope or long strips of cloth and tighten

Illustration 4.1
Regluing leg stretcher

with a tourniquet to hold the chair tightly together until it dries. (See illustration 4.1.) There are books in most libraries that will teach you all you need to know about furniture repair and upholstering and slipcovering. This knowledge will give you confidence to shop in thrift stores, knowing an item doesn't have to be perfect to meet your needs.

Thrift stores are a great source for decorative details and objects for carrying out a particular theme. But you need to keep an open mind. Remember, an item does not have to be used for its original purpose. A wicker fishing creel (if you could find one) doesn't have to be used as a fishing creel. They are valued today as containers for floral arrangements, magazine or mail holders, or just as decorative items in a room with an outdoor or masculine feel.

You might find a piece of furniture that has nice detail, but it might be the wrong color. Spray paint and some stencils will fix that quickly. One woman bought all the small tables she could find. After painting them stark white, she decorated them with decoupage or stenciled designs. She then resold them, for a nice profit, to boutiques and specialty shops.

Fabrics can also be recycled and used for purposes other than their original intent. Jo recently turned a delicate embroidered piece she found many years ago into a decorative sofa pillow. She sewed the piece onto blue-and-white striped fabric to stabilize it and to create a border. She then sewed wide, white rickrack around the edge of the embroidered piece. She added thick white fringe to the outer edge, then sewed the front and back of the pillow together. Lastly she stuffed her new pillow cover with an old sofa pillow she no longer liked, and voilà, a decorator touch for pennies.

Gwen learned to buy a fabric piece that pleases her eye if the price is right, even if she has no immediate plans for it. An opportunity to use it will come along eventually. Such was the case with a white linen tablecloth dripping with real Brussels lace—the old-fashioned kind—that she spotted in a thrift shop. The piece had some stains, so she soaked it in Rit color remover to get them out. Some of the lace had come apart. She reworked the stitches with fine crochet thread. It was time-consuming, but the end result was a beautiful piece that she used first on a canopy bed and is now using as a half canopy hung against a dark wall. The dark color behind the lace shows off the pattern beautifully. Her tablecloth found a whole new life.

If it's inexpensive (a shoestring decorator's dream) and it pleases you, buy it, but don't put it away and forget it. Chances are that beautiful piece that pleases you will eventually find a place in your home as a decorative item. Lovely handkerchiefs with either handmade or machine-lace edgings can be used as pillow covers, as Jo has used hers, or can be starched and used as doilies or even framed as pictures. Silk or acrylic scarves intended as accessories for dresses and suits can be easily converted to decorative pillows or window hangings.

Thrift shops are also a great source for starting or adding to collections. Gwen has added many items to her red plate collection. Jo saw so many pretty china teacup saucers in these stores that she began to collect them. You will find candlesticks, statuary, typewriters, cameras, artwork of all kinds, figurines, jewelry, boxes, old hats and gloves, boudoir accessories, desk accessories, kitchen gadgets, books, records, tapes, vases, mugs, and so many other items. Some will tickle your funny bone, others will bring back memories. Some will inspire the collector in you, and others will simply confound you.

Looking for decorative accessories and objects for our homes is an ongoing hobby for both of us. (And we love to go shopping together.) But both of us have very high standards about quality. We want classy and classic homes, not homes that are simply a place for a collection of junk. *Shopping junk stores does not mean you have to have a junky-looking home.*

Resale Shops

Jo doesn't shop at these places very often because generally their prices are too high. However, she found the perfect set of Noritaki china she'd wanted for years at an estate sale store in Portland. It was a complete set for eight, for about $120. (Then Jo's parents found an almost identical set, with service for twelve and all the serving pieces, at a garage sale, and they paid only $75. A few years later, they donated that to Jo's collection!)

Generally at resale shops, the proprietor is selling on consignment or he has bought the items at estate and yard sales and is marking up to cover his overhead and make a profit. However, you may be able to dicker over prices here. As with thrift stores, check carefully for quality. Generally, items don't move as fast as they do in thrift stores, so you can go home and think about something before buying.

The want ads in your local newspaper are a great substitute for the resale shop—you eliminate the middle man. By calling and asking the right questions, you can decide if you want to go and see the item or not. If you say you're going, be courteous and show up. Before you call, make a list of questions so you don't forget something important. Here are some important questions to ask:

- How old is it?
- What color is it?
- What shape is it in? Does it have any stains, breaks, or scratches?
- What is the name of the manufacturer?
- What are the dimensions?
- How firm is the price?
- Why are you getting rid of it? (You want to know how anxious they are to sell.)
- Are all the pieces there (for example, all the leaves for a table)?
- Are any others interested in it?

- Is it real wood? What kind of upholstery fabric? Are any springs sprung?
- Has it been left outside?
- Does anyone in the household smoke? (The smell is hard to get out of some things.)

Bartering or Trading

This is a fun pastime for the adventurous soul. There is a whole subculture that wants to trade skill for things. We won't delve into that. However, keep in mind that we barter all the time: "I'll watch your kids today for two hours if you will watch mine tomorrow for two hours." Jo's brother, who is an architect, helped his sister and her husband design their dream home. In exchange, the sister's husband built an entire wall of shelves and cupboards for the brother's family room.

Do you have a skill or something of value to trade with someone? One of Jo's friends wallpapered another friend's kitchen in exchange for piano lessons. A handyman may be willing to build a piece of furniture for you if you do his taxes, clean his house, or watch his kids. Want ads sometimes have opportunities for barter or trades. But the best source is the people you know. Talk with your friends at church, coworkers, neighbors, and others to discover what their needs and skills are. That's the family of Christ working together.

A word to the wise, though. If you are exchanging money, wait until all the money is there before making the transaction. Never get involved in a monthly payment plan with a friend. Too often the borrower will come up with many reasons and emergencies that prevent making that month's payment. As a friend, you will be expected to "understand." Tell the friend that you will hold the item until all the money is saved up, but don't hand over the item until then. You are putting a friendship in danger when someone owes you money. This works the other way too. Wait until you have all the cash you need before taking possession of something.

Garage, Barn, and Yard Sales

These sales occur throughout the country, though each area seems to call them by a different name. They're all pretty much the same—people trying to get rid of unwanted stuff and make a dollar or two. You might want to hold one of these sales yourself, to make a few dollars to go toward a purchase for decorating your home.

Jo enjoys studying the garage sale ads in the paper. With map in hand, she plans her garage sale route. If you see an ad for a really hot item, plan to get there as it opens or it will be gone. Inevitably, there are unadvertised sales along the way. Jo was looking for an area rug for under her dining room table. She found the perfect one, lying in the sun on a driveway at an unadvertised garage sale.

Bring cash to these sales, both to limit your spending and to make buying easier and quicker. (Thankfully, we've yet to see a garage sale that took plastic.) Most sellers are willing to come down in prices. If you are the first buyer and it's early in the day, they may take your name and number and call you later if a better deal doesn't come along. Sellers are more anxious to sell when the sale is almost over, because no one wants to cart their junk back into the house.

If you buy a big item and need to come back with a truck later to haul it away, help the sellers move it out of sight and put a "sold" sign on it. Exchange names and phone numbers in case something happens. Again, be careful about quality. Bring along anything you want to match and a tape measure.

Also, keep an eye out in your neighborhood. Don't be shy about stopping when you see an item you want on the curb in front of a neighbor's home. Vicki saw a white wicker chair with the trash at a neighbor's home. The seat was caved in, but she put it under a tree in her front yard and decorated it with a pot of petunias. It looks charming. If you're not sure it's really trash, ring the doorbell and ask.

Outlets, Warehouse Sales, and Markdown Rooms

Outlet malls have exploded in the last ten years. Initially they had great prices, and some still do, but now they are often no better than sale prices at local retail stores. If you use outlet stores, shop first at quality retail stores so you know good quality when you see it and what prices you should expect. The best time to visit an outlet store is during a sale.

Warehouse sales are sometimes just come-ons, but they're worth checking out. Don't get your hopes up that you will find exactly what you want, but the prices are generally great. Jo and Al bought their television and VCR at half price thirteen years ago at a two-day warehouse sale. Sometimes the merchandise is damaged; sometimes they're selling outdated inventory or orders that were never picked up. Furniture that was made wrong and has to be reordered is often sold for cost. Jo's family room sectional couch was initially delivered with the extension on the wrong side and had to be reordered. She saw it for sale on the warehouse floor a few weeks later.

Some stores have a markdown room with the same kinds of rejects mentioned above. They might also include furniture that has been on the floor for a while and may look a little faded or worn. These rooms aren't easy to find, so call around to see which stores have them. While you're on the phone, ask if the item you want is there and save more money by not driving from store to store.

We can't stress enough the importance of having a plan as you shop at thrift stores, yard sales, and markdown rooms. You need to know what you are shopping for. That great buy on a contemporary dining table will be a bad buy if you have decided to go with a traditional style; nothing else in the dining room will look good with it. We cannot stress enough the importance of not guessing whether something will match. Carry with you paint chips, a tiny piece of carpet, or fabric swatches. Keep that small tape measure with you at all times. If you know that today you will be shopping for a chair to coordinate with a sofa,

don't be shy about carrying a sofa cushion or pillow made of the same fabric. You can leave it in the car until you find something; then go get it to double-check if it matches. Never rely on your memory for color—you will almost certainly be wrong.

If you think all of this seems like a time-consuming activity, you're right! If you are intent on decorating on a shoestring, you need to do a lot of research—it just feels like shopping. Have patience and don't rush into things. Wait to buy until you find exactly what you want, and don't waste time and money on something cheaply made, just because you think it "will do." You can live a long time without a sofa. Even your company will understand. (Though you *so* wanted to get a sofa before they arrived!) Staying within your budget and waiting for exactly what you need is more pleasing to God than going into debt or making foolish purchases.

Shoestring Tips

- Read the want ads daily to know the market for the items you need.
- Be brave and bargain when buying at garage sales and through want ads. (A good rule of thumb is to offer 75 percent of the asking price.)
- Always be very personable when negotiating. People like to give nice people a good deal.
- Look beyond coats of paint on wood furniture.
- For information on how to fix furniture, check your local library.

CHAPTER 5

A New Way of Looking at It

Before you head out to shop—even to shop at thrift stores—stop! You may already have what you need right in your home. Perhaps all you need is a new way of looking at what you have. Read this chapter and then open all your closet and cupboard doors and see what's stored away. Go down to the basement or out to the garage. Stand back and look at everything you have in a new way. Sometimes all we need is God to open our eyes to see the possibilities.

If you're really stuck, brainstorm with family members and friends about how to solve a particular decorating problem. In all of life a "can-do" attitude is valuable, and here's a good place to learn it. You will be surprised what you can dream up and do. We encourage you to learn new skills and to look at things in new ways. Decorating is fun and not nearly as serious and intimidating as some of you think. You can do it!

Thrift is not a one-time event. It's a way of life. So put on your thinking caps about what you already have. For example, what would happen if you moved your long bedroom dresser out of your overcrowded bedroom and into the living room? The drawers provide storage, and the top is a place to display pretty collectibles. What would happen if you placed it behind a sofa to use as a sofa table? It could hold a lamp, reading material, collectibles, or a lovely floral arrangement. You could still use it for storage, even putting your clothes in the drawers if you didn't mind carrying them to the bedroom for dressing.

Let's take that same long dresser and put it in a home office. Now it has just become a credenza. If you are concerned about scratching the top, have a piece of glass cut to fit. You can afford it; you just saved yourself a lot of money by not going out to buy a credenza.

Now, for fun, let's put it in the dining room. Aha! A sideboard and extra storage to boot. Maybe it's scratched and old, and you're tired of it anyway. Paint it and put it in a nursery. You might even be able to use it for a changing table. Is it too short? Legs are available at the hardware store. Need it lower? Replace the legs with shorter ones or with wheels or do without.

Do you see the possibilities? Just for fun, pick a piece of furniture and think of three different ways it might be used in three different rooms.

Think about What You Own

As in the example given above, sometimes all we have to do to satisfy our decorating needs is to step back and look at what we have in a new way. It may be as simple as moving a piece of furniture from one room to another. It may mean re-upholstering or slipcovering an existing piece of furniture, but only if it is well made and worth the time and expense. It may be painting, stenciling, or decoupaging an item that just would-n't fit in a room and turning it into a decorator piece.

Start by identifying the absolute essentials of what you need. Then look around to see what meets those requirements. For example, your specific need may be storage of certain di-mensions, a place to display a collection, or merely something tall to add height in a room. Many things may meet your re-quirements even though they were not created for the purpose you have in mind.

Perhaps the best way to help you catch the vision of this new thinking is to give several examples of easy-to-do projects.

Chests of Drawers

Got an old chest of drawers? Here are some things you can do with it.

Refinish it:
- Paint it all one color or all white.
- Sponge paint it.
- Marbleize it.

- Stencil or paint stripes, flowers, garden scenes, landscapes, trees, sporting events, angels, a night sky, etc.
- Strip it and refinish it in a natural-wood look.
- Do fake inlay looks with stains.
- Give it a bleached-wood finish.
- Antique it and replace the pulls.
- Paint a scene on each drawer.

In the dining room:
- Top it with a tea set.
- Top it with a collection—teapots, pictures, trays.
- Use it to store table linens, silver, china.
- Use it as a sideboard.

In the family or living room:
- Put the TV on top.
- Store videos in drawers, spine side up.
- Store games, hobby items, out-of-season things.
- Display a collection.
- Use it to fill up a corner.
- Top it with plants, photos, candles, a lamp, art objects.

In the entryway:
- Top it with collectibles and a mirror on the wall above.
- Let pretty linens and laces spill from the drawers.
- Put a tray on top for keys.

Drop-Leaf Tables

Let's do the same exercise with a drop-leaf table. Jo found one in a used furniture store more than twenty years ago. She has nicknamed it "The Little Drop-Leaf Table That Could."

At first it was the kitchen table in a tiny apartment. Jo and her housemate, Judy, purchased the table together for fifteen dollars. They disliked the finish, so they stripped, stained, and varnished it. It was agreed that whoever married first surrendered the table to the other. Jo held out the longest, so she now owns it.

That little table lived in two more apartment kitchens before Al and Jo moved to Portland, Oregon. The large apartment they rented there had room for a "real" table, so they bought a nice, big table for their dining room and put the little drop-leaf table back in the kitchen for general kitchen use.

Later in their first house, the drop-leaf table was used to divide the entry space from the rest of the living room. Sometimes they moved it around for other uses, such as a place to put their TV or a sofa table with pretty plants on it. That little table has been used as a place to sew and do projects, as a table in the breakfast room, and has been in almost every room of the homes the Janssens have owned. It is still in use, and it still looks good.

Gwen also has a drop-leaf table that she purchased for fifteen dollars. When Gwen bought the table at a garage sale, it had about twenty coats of paint on it. It took her weeks to peel off all the paint. She tried using a chemical paint stripper, but the paint was so thick it wouldn't all come off in a single operation. Then she rented a paint-stripping tool—it looks something like a hair dryer and throws a powerfully hot stream of air. It literally blisters the paint so that it can be removed with a flat-bladed spackling knife. (If you use one of these be extremely careful. Paint is not the only thing it will blister—tender skin will burn in a second. Follow instructions carefully for the use of such a tool.) And that was only the top. The legs were a nightmare, but when she got all the paint off, she stained the table and then applied polyurethane. It has been in constant use ever since as a table for eating.

Chandeliers

In Jo's dining room is a chandelier that she would not have chosen. It has brushed brass, smoky bronze globes—1978 chic. To disguise it, she removed the smoky bronze globes and replaced the candle-flame bulbs with round ones. Then she covered small, inexpensive shades made for chandeliers with linen fabric and put them on the bulb lights. Finally, she wove silk ivy around the brass and up the chain. Now it fits into her garden theme, and all for pennies.

Consider these other ways to disguise distasteful chandeliers:

- Make or remake shades to cover bare bulbs.
- Paint the fixture with a metal finish found in hobby stores or paint it white.
- Cover the whole thing with fabric.
- Cover it with silk plants.
- Remove shades or globes and use decorative bulbs.
- Watch thrift shops for globes that fit your decor.

If it is too ugly to disguise, consider these options:

- Buy another one. Watch thrift and resale shops for chandeliers. Gwen recently bought one with brass, glass, and candles for ten dollars.
- Make a chandelier by purchasing a pleated shade with some flair and fit it with a light socket and chain. Screw in a big round globe and install a dimmer switch to create a lovely mood.
- Look for other items that could be used as a chandelier. If you are into contemporary, perhaps some of the industrial fixtures used in factories and workshops would be perfect for your look. Spray paint the metal shade of your fixture black, white, or another color to complement your decor.

Bookcases

Bookcases are useful in home decorating because they can be used to store and display everything from the books for which they were intended to toys. If they are tall, they can add height to a room. Bookcases are hard to find in thrift shops. They are snatched up instantly or are used by store personnel for displaying books and items. So keep your eyes open wide when shopping for bookcases. This is one of the times it pays to know when the furniture shipments come to your thrift shop—be there as the truck is being unloaded.

We are not sure you can have too many bookcases because they are so useful. Here are some ideas, and we're sure you'll think of many more.

- Tall bookcases can be used as room dividers. If the backs are not finished, you may want to cover them with fabric, wallpaper, or paint to match the room they face.
- Short ones can be used under a window as a window seat or behind a sofa as a sofa table that also keeps reading material close by.
- Use a short bookcase beside your bed for a bedside table.
- Put a tall, skinny one in the bathroom as a place to store towels and baskets of personal items for family members.
- Use one in a corner and fill it with plants and a collection.
- Put one in the closet for extra storage.
- In the hallway, a bookcase can hold decorative items, hatboxes for storing gloves and scarves, or a tray for keys.
- Set one on top of a table or desk to make a hutch.
- Use a pair of short ones for a table base.
- Over a bed, bookcases can function as a storage headboard.
- Install doors on your bookcase, and you'll have a storage cabinet.
- Paint the doors you've installed and the bookshelves to create a dollhouse for a little girl's room. Or paint the whole thing to function as a city, and use it as storage for your son's tiny toy trucks and cars.
- When a bookcase is hopelessly ugly, don't throw it out. Send it to the garage, basement, garden shed, back porch, or anywhere you need storage.

Sewing Machine Cabinets

We often see old sewing machine cabinets with and without sewing machines in them. We're not interested in the sewing machine; it's the cabinet we're after. These cabinets are often in terrible condition and desperately need refinishing.

Take a good look at a cabinet you find and think what it might become in your home:

- a bedside table
- an entry table
- a small, dining room sideboard
- a place to display a silver tea set, plants, or a collection
- a chairside table to hold a lamp and reading material
- in a corner as a decorative item

Old TV Cabinets

Old TV cabinets are well made and often of lovely design. Jo found a use for one in her first home. She needed a place to store her TV and stereo equipment out of sight, but still in her little living/family room. She found an old TV cabinet in a thrift shop. The shop owner let her have it cheap because no one else saw any potential in it. It was big and had built-in shelves behind the door.

Jo took out the old TV and stripped the wood, thinking she had a cherry cabinet. Surprise! It had only been stained to look like beautiful wood grain. (Sometimes that happens.) It was solid wood, but nothing special. So Jo changed her plans and painted it white to match the room's walls. She put it in the corner of the room, and it looked built-in. It housed the Janssen's stereo system and records behind doors for many years.

Sofas

Need a sofa? Turn a single bed into one by slipping on a cover that reaches the floor and filling it with big, comfy pillows. Use it in a family room.

Or nail together a simple platform—a box with a top. Paint the base, or cover it with fabric. Cover a thick, foam pad or a twin mattress with a decorator fabric, and put it on top of the platform. Fill the "sofa" with pretty pillows.

Tables

Use a plain door from a lumberyard or home center. Put it on some kind of sturdy base. Fasten the top to the base by attaching it with angle braces. Cover it with a floor-length skirt and you have an instant table.

In fact, a floor-length skirt can cover most any table. Check out shoestring places for those detachable legs that can be screwed into a flat surface to make a table, or buy the legs and a particleboard top at a home improvement store.

Purchase an inexpensive folding table at a discount store. Those tables are solid and cost about thirty dollars. That's not very much for a lovely dining room table. A sturdy but ugly old table with a plastic top and metal legs will work just fine. All of these options work if you cover them with a floor-length skirt and top them with a piece of glass. No one needs to know what's underneath.

Accessory Items

This is where the fun really begins, because a new use for an old item can be as original as the person making the selection. Here are a few ideas to get your creative juices flowing:

- Instead of folding and storing those wonderful gift bags, use them to store items. A small one holds envelopes on a desk. Use one in the bathroom to store extra cosmetic items. Put them on top of kitchen cupboards to store staple items when space is at a premium. Put one beside your bed to hold reading material.
- Use a jar, basket, teapot, jug, pitcher, cup, tin, or an old pot for a vase.
- Need a planter? Use a basket, coal scuttle, metal box, wooden box, or can—there's good use for all those big popcorn tins you get at Christmas.
- Table napkins can become place mats, doilies, pillows, chair arm covers, bookshelf dressing, lamp covers, tiebacks for curtains, and can even be used as napkins.
- Hankies with beautiful lace and edgings can be used as doilies, framed as wall art, sewn on pillows, or used as a hankie.

- Use blankets, quilts, sheets, tablecloths, clothing, or any fabric you like to make slipcovers, pillows, lamp shade covers, chair pads, table napkins, curtain tiebacks, footstool covers, window valances, quilts, table runners, or covers for books and boxes.
- Cut old clothes into strips for braid rugs.
- Buy formal and bridesmaid dresses at thrift shops and use the fabric and lace for decorative pillows.
- Scour fabric store closeout bins for fabrics that fit your theme and please you. Use them to cover a headboard, make tablecloths and napkins, line baskets, cover flowerpots, make a bed ruffle, create big bows to put anywhere, line a quilt, make pillows, or curtains. Make quilts or wall hangings, use as a throw for a chair or sofa, line a box or drawer, cover a frame, create a desk set, cover a bulletin board, create unique Christmas stockings, or decoupage fabric onto a lamp, bowl, or box.

Something-from-Nothing Ideas

Jo saw some pretty coasters in a catalog that had a needle-point floral design. She dug down in her needlework basket and found some cross-stitch fabric and leftover embroidery floss. She even found some floral designs left over from other projects she had done. She created six very pretty coaster designs on four-inch squares of fabric. Then she trimmed them with piping and lined them with other scraps for some lovely, washable coasters.

To store the coasters, Jo wanted a pretty little basket. She saw one in an ad but didn't order it. She found a basket with a lid on sale for fifty cents. She painted it white and stenciled a floral design on it (the stencil and paint were also left over from other projects). Then she tucked in the coasters and set the whole thing in her living room where it fits perfectly.

Gwen had an ugly, wrought-iron Mediterranean-style lamp. She went to a barn sale and bought six books of the kind no one could pay you to read, but with nice bindings in attractive colors. She disassembled the lamp, then drilled a hole through each book and inserted the lamp's rod through all the books to make a creative lamp for her writer's desk.

Jo took a stack of coffee table books and topped them with a napkin with pretty cutwork and a tray to create a chairside table. To top it, she added a favorite teacup. Gwen created a similar "table" by using a stack of old, leather-bound encyclopedias and topped it with a piece of beveled glass.

Gwen got tired of her necklace chains becoming all tangled. She put a belt hook—the kind that has about fifteen hooks in a straight row—in the closet and hangs her necklaces there for quick selection when she's dressing in the morning. A tie rack (the expandable kind) would work as well.

Coffee Tables

To make a coffee table you just need something sturdy for the base and a top. Most anything will work.

- Find an old stump or a piece of driftwood. Clean it thoroughly to remove all soil. Then have it cut so that the top is perfectly level. Add a piece of thick bevel-edged glass.
- Clean a birdbath and top it with glass. You could even put decorative items or flowers in the birdbath under the glass.
- Use a pair of pedestals, planters, or old-fashioned wooden crates.

- Use a lobster pot, old-fashioned nail kegs, or sturdy baskets.
- Top a small chest of drawers with glass or a board finished to look like granite or marble.
- Stack up old bricks.

Lighting

- Paint a coffee can and put a light socket through the bottom of it to make a real "can" light. Use it for spot lighting by hanging it from the ceiling, or prop it on a brick behind a plant for dramatic back lighting.
- Make a coffee table appear to float by placing a light under it.
- Use a lamp kit to turn any sturdy item into a lamp base. One of Gwen's favorite lamps—purchased ready-made (but probably homemade) in a thrift shop—is a pewter pitcher on a base. She tucked green silk plants into the top of the jug and added a pleated print shade she also found in a thrift shop. Other lamp base ideas: baskets, toys, sports equipment, wooden boxes, vases, flowerpots, birdhouses, blocks of wood, figurines, statues, lawn ornaments, dolls, stuffed animals, stacks of books, trophies, jars (filled with rocks, jelly beans, or seashells), tins, jugs, bottles, antique cameras, or radios.

Aids for Home Decorating

Hook and Loop Tape

Hook and loop tape is sold under the brand name of Velcro. It can be purchased at hardware and fabric stores. This stuff is today's gift to home decorators. Use it to:

- Attach fringe or trim to the edges of fireplace mantels and shelves.
- Attach a picture frame to the bathroom mirror. Notch on the underside of the frame the places where you must accommodate the clips that hold the mirror in place. For added strength, staple the tape to the back of the picture frame.
- Add a temporary wall covering by attaching lengths of fabric to the walls.
- Add a skirt to a pedestal sink.
- Attach a skirt to a tabletop to make a skirt vanity.

Monofilament (Fishing) Line

Monofilament fishing line can be purchased at hardware and sporting goods stores. If you are living in an apartment and the owners frown on holes in the walls, you can use monofilament line to do a number of decorating projects. Here's how: Put tiny nails or screw eyes at the juncture where ceiling and walls come together. (These can be filled with white toothpaste when you leave.) Hang monofilament line from these nails to accomplish these and other projects:

- Hang wall art by attaching monofilament line to the hanging clips on wire of picture frames.
- For drapes and curtains, make a hem pocket in the short edge of lengths of fabric. Insert a dowel and hang the dowel using the monofilament line. (See illustration 5.1.)
- Create all kinds of wonderful window treatments by gathering a long length of fabric and catching it up and fastening it with the transparent line.

Spring Tension Rods

These rods can be purchased anywhere curtains are sold as well as in hardware stores. They are also called tension rods and are long curtain rods with a spring built into them. They are used between two hard surfaces and can be adjusted to different widths. No hardware is needed for installation. This is another gift to decorators from modern technology.

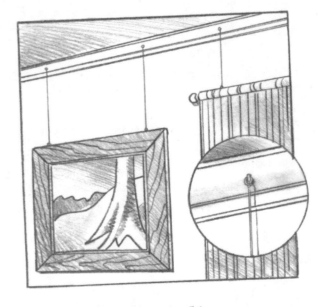

Illustration 5.1
Hanging with monofilament line

- Use a tension rod in the bathroom to create a lovely look around your bathtub. Even if you have glass doors, soften the look by putting up a lace curtain, or by adding a topper using another spring tension rod.
- Thread tension rods through a fabric panel to cover a wall. You can even shirr the fabric onto the rod for fullness.
- You can use a spring tension rod between any two sturdy surfaces. Gwen put a spring tension rod between two bookcases flanking a window and put up a favorite lace topper to soften the look of the room.
- Put up a series of spring tension rods in a closet to hang table linens.
- Get good spring tension rods and hang on to them when you move. They will be used again somewhere else.

We have only begun to scratch the surface of looking at what you have and what you can find in a new way. The most exciting thing is that none of us see things in the same way, and that opens the door to all kinds of wonderful, creative thinking about decorating. You, too, can become the home decorator about whom people say, "How did she ever think of that? What a wonderful, creative solution! I think I'll try that."

CHAPTER 6

Color Your Shoestring

When Jo and her family first entered their present home they felt overwhelmed by a feeling of cavelike gloom. The linoleum, doors, woodwork, and bookshelves were all the color of dark chocolate. The heavy gold drapes over two windows blocked most of the light the area desperately needed. No wonder this home had been on the market for so long!

The colors in our homes set the mood and say something about us. They can convey seriousness, gloom, lightheartedness, cheerfulness, grandeur, playfulness, or peacefulness. Jo did not want to live with the oppressing darkness of her new home, so she immediately began to transform all the dark brown surfaces into cheerful white. The entry now seems spacious, bright, and inviting. Color made the difference.

Color Is Important

In recent years psychologists have discovered that we respond to color in specific ways. Let's examine how color affects our mood.

Neutral Colors

Neutral colors give a room a feeling of peace and harmony. The wide range of neutral colors include khaki, tan, taupe, beige, white, gray, and black. Lighter neutral colors such as white, beige, and light gray are excellent colors against which to display fabrics, paintings, accessories, and furnishings. Several of Gwen's houses have had all-white bathrooms. The up side of white bathrooms is that they are easy to redecorate by changing the shower curtain, window topper, bath rugs, and towels. In a few minutes you can have a completely new look. The down side is that white bathrooms have to be kept clean—very clean. Every bit of dust, soap scum, or spilled cosmetics shows.

Neutral colors create a roomy feeling because they recede visually. They make walls and furniture look farther away than they actually are. White and other pale neutrals reflect light and make a small room look bigger. Wallpaper in tiny, neutral-colored prints also visually extends the size of the room. On the other hand, a dark, neutral color absorbs light and makes a room look small. Sponging a slightly darker shade of the same basic wall color can add texture, interest, and soften neutrals.

Light Colors

Pink is calming and is often used in hospitals and wards for the mentally ill. Pastels provide a soft look. They are easy to live with and are therefore often chosen as background colors.

Bright Colors

Bright colors are exuberant and exciting. They include intense shades of blue, yellow, and red as well as black and white. In most cases they should be used with restraint because in a group they can overwhelm.

Dark colors

Green, purple, maroon, and navy blue are regal, having a dignified air and reminding us of royalty. You might want to reserve these colors for more formal rooms.

Dull Colors

These are colors that have been grayed to a mellow hue. Dusty pink, taupe brown, and various shades of gray can evoke a quiet, contemplative mood. They often become nondescript unless they are linked with bright accents.

Cool Colors

Cool colors run from green to violet and include blue and gray. These are calming and cooling colors. They make us think of water, snow, and ice. Some cool colors—blues and grays—will warm considerably with a dash of red in them. Blues, greens, and violets are called receding colors and make a room seem larger and cooler. These colors speak to us of nature and tranquillity.

Warm Colors

These range from red to yellow on the color wheel. They demand attention, lend excitement, "heat up" the coldest of rooms, and always dominate a color scheme. Psychologists say they may even increase our drive and help us work faster. They are called advancing colors and make a room seem smaller.

Natural Colors

Natural colors are also called earth tones. They blend many hues so that you have a mahogany brown, a burnt orange, a terra-cotta red. Brown reminds us of rich, fertile soil. These colors are often muted. They provide a soothing, rich look and combine well with natural woods and leathers.

Surprising Colors

Some colors are shocking, hot, and attention-getting. Neon colors and colors with no gray or brown to tone them down are attention getters. Sometimes the colors are surprising because of the way they are paired (i.e., magenta with purple).

No Color

We tend to see white as the absence of color (it actually consists of all colors). It expresses innocence and purity. Black is the color of night, death, and evil on one hand and yet can speak of elegance and wealth (i.e., little black dresses, long black limousines).

Choosing a Color Scheme

There are two ways to approach the decision of a successful color scheme for your rooms. One is to start from scratch and learn about color yourself. We will teach you how to use a color wheel to aid you in that process. The second way is to use tried–and–true color schemes that others have perfected. We can reap the benefits of what artists and designers have learned. We will show you how to use someone else's research and experimentation. Let's start by discussing the color wheel. A sample is printed on the inside back cover of this book. You might also locate one at your local paint or decorating retailer.

The Color Wheel

The color wheel is based on the three *primary* colors: red, blue, and yellow. Right in the middle between those primary colors are the *secondary* colors, which are made by mixing equal parts of the primary colors: green between blue and yellow, orange between yellow and red, and violet between red and blue.

Think of a clock face with red at the top of the wheel, at "twelve o'clock." Think of yellow at 4:00 and blue at 8:00. At 2:00, you'll find orange, made from red and yellow. Continuing on around the circle, yellow and blue make green at 6:00, blue and red make violet at 10:00.

The next colors to examine are the *tertiary* colors that you get when you mix a primary color with its nearest secondary color. Take yellow and its nearest secondary colors: on the green side of yellow you get yellow-green; on the other side you

get yellow-orange. The other tertiary colors are blue-green, red-orange, red-violet, and blue-violet.

Obviously, the color wheel doesn't represent all colors. An infinite number of variations of all these colors can be created by adding different amounts of white, black, or gray to them. For example, if white is added to red, pink is created. Add black to red and maroon is the result. Add grey to red and you get rose. This will work not only for the primary colors, but for the secondary and tertiary colors as well. The resulting colors will vary in brightness and intensity depending on how much or little white, black, or grey is added.

Tried–and–True Color Schemes

Using the color wheel, you can make your own successful color schemes. There are traditional ways of doing this, each with its own term and recipe for success.

Contrasting or complementary colors

These are the colors that are directly opposite each other on the color wheel (i.e., red and green). In a contrasting color scheme, you may choose one color as the main one and the other as an accent or secondary color.

Split-complementary

This is closely related to the complementary scheme. You use complementary colors plus the tertiary colors surrounding one of the complementary colors. For example, if red is your first color choice, choose green as a complementary color and the tertiary colors of yellow-green and blue-green.

Analogous

To achieve this scheme, begin with a primary color, then use the tertiary colors on either side of it. An example of this is using yellow, yellow-orange, and yellow-green together.

Triad

This scheme uses any three colors of equal distance from one another on the color wheel (i.e., the classic kids' room combination of red, yellow, and blue).

Monochromatic

The prefix *mono* means one, so a monochromatic color scheme is based on shades of one color. For example, you could paint the walls of a room light mint green. The flooring could be dark forest green, and the furniture a patterned, medium green.

A monochromatic color scheme is excellent for visually pushing the walls back. To achieve a visually spacious room, paint the walls, woodwork, and baseboards in a matching color. Then hang draperies that match the wall color. The room will instantly appear larger.

Monochromatic color schemes don't have to be boring. Using new glazing techniques, two shades of the same color can be sponged on to the walls to add visual dimension, texture, and interest. Monochromatic color schemes give a wonderful backdrop for paintings, rugs, and other decorative items. The effect can be quite dramatic.

Shortcut Methods for Choosing a Color Scheme

Wasn't it nice for all those generations of artists and decorators to leave us thousands of pictures we can now see in museums, magazines, and books? What a wealth of ideas and design wisdom from which to draw. Let's peek at some of their formulas for successful color scheming.

The easiest one is white and any color. Take a look at all of your stuff. Is there one color you use a lot? Do you have quite a few things that are green on a white background? Try a green-and-white color scheme.

Or let someone else's success inspire you. Copy a room you really like from a magazine or a home you've seen. Jo saw a picture in a magazine of an office painted dark red. The furniture and accessories were white. On the floor was a dark red oriental rug. Jo tore out the page and put it in her file. She knew she had everything needed for this room except an office with red walls. When the Janssens moved to Colorado, she created her red office. It looks just as good as the magazine version. (Her husband thinks it's better!)

Another technique is to find a fabric or wallpaper you really love and use those colors in the same proportions. Picture a flowery lilac print on a white background used as a bedspread. Give the room a white background, and add some lilac colored items. Use green (from lilac leaves in the print) as an accent.

Look for inspiration from a picture, plate, quilt, art, pillow, or anything, and copy that for your color scheme. Use the colors in the same proportions for your room.

Here are some cheap and easy ways to choose a color scheme:

- Use one color in all its different shades.
- Use a neutral in many textures.
- Use just the primary colors.
- Use a neutral and one color as a backdrop for art, collections, or mementos from your travels.

If you're not sure whether or not a color will work in a room, or even if you will like it, try it in small doses first. Perhaps a pillow or a poster with those colors could be put in the room for a while to test it.

Visit Your Paint Store

Paint stores are a marvelous place to visit. Many of them have on-site interior decorators to help you. They have paint cards that give you a color with all its tints and shades. The cards often include complementary accent colors. In addition, there are decorating booklets, idea brochures, and more; Gwen once even received a hardback book about draperies and color.

If you lack inspiration, paint stores often have fabric swatches, wallpaper galore, stencils and stenciling equipment, and instructions and equipment for creating decorative paint surfaces. Many of them also have carpeting and tile of all kinds.

If you are unsure, pick a paper you love and work backward, matching colors found in that wallpaper. Someone has paid designers thousands of dollars to design these decorative papers. These are highly schooled and highly skilled people. You don't have to reinvent the color wheel. It's all right to copy color schemes from the experts.

Pattern, Solids, Stripes, and Prints

Author Patsy Clairmont has a home that is a delight to the eye.[1] She has boldly mixed stripes, solids, and prints, and the result is warm and pleasing. Her guest bedroom is done in blue and white with yellow as the accent color, a wonderful color complement to the Victorian oak furniture in the room.

The top half of the room is papered with a print of small, blue bows on a white background. The bottom half is blue, yellow, and white stripes. The top and bottom wallpapers are divided by a chair-rail-height border paper in a print.

In the corner of the room is a wonderful, overstuffed chair in a multicolored floral print of tiny flowers. On the floor is a blue, yellow, and white hooked area rug. The bedding is a mixture of checks in blue, yellow, and white.

You, too, can successfully mix stripes, prints, checks, plaids, and solids. A good way to learn how to mix colors and prints is to look in wallpaper books for matching papers and fabrics. One company's display ad shows a bold blue-and-white stripe on the walls and covering chairs in a tiny bedroom. At the window is a poufed Austrian shade in a tiny blue-and-white print. A larger print blue-and-white border is used as a chair rail. All of these are in the same shade of blue and white. Now toss in a big, floral print in hat boxes and cushions—wonderful!

Gwen once decorated a bedroom mixing several different patterns in similar shades. She put raspberry pink carpeting on the floor and used blue-and-white-striped chintz for a sofa in the room, a bed skirt, and to cover a round table all the way to the floor. Then she made a duvet of a floral that had blue ribbons as part of the print. Her sheets were in pinks and blues. She filled the striped sofa with print pillows. An adjoining bathroom had blue-and-white-striped towels. Matching chairs in a tiny blue-and-pink print sat in the bay window in the room. The room was a delight.

When you play with prints in a room, it is important to remember that there needs to be one dominant color and one dominant print. The room gets restless if two or more are represented equally. Balance the use of a strong print with a triangular placement around a room—use it in at least three different areas of the room.

There are some tried and true formulas for successfully mixing prints that anyone can do. An easy one is to use one print, check, or plaid in various scales—small, medium, and large—throughout the room. Jo's sister used orange gingham checks in different scales throughout her sewing room with charming results.

Another easy way to create a mix is to begin with a print for a large item, such as a sofa or draperies. Then pick out one main color in the print. Use that color in a stripe or check elsewhere in the room. Also use it in a subtle, dot-like print on a neutral background. A variation of this combines a print with a solid in the dominant color in the print.

Be careful, though, when mixing prints not to mix two large prints in the same room. They will war with each other. You can use different prints with the same colors together—just make sure one of them dominates. And don't forget about the already mixed designer fabrics and wallpapers that are chosen for you. They are more expensive, but the mixing and choosing is foolproof.

Combining Colors in a Room

Color—the amounts and combinations used—will have a powerful impact on the overall look of a room. Here are some basics to remember about color:

- Colors directly opposite on the color wheel will contrast more than if one color is played against a lighter shade of the contrasting color. For example, a true green contrasted against a true red appears brighter than it does against a lighter shade of red such as pink.
- A color appears brighter as it is reflected from one surface to another surface of the same color. So painting one wall green will not have as much impact as painting all four walls of the room green. The green from each wall will reflect on the other walls and intensify the color.

- Color will appear differently on different walls because of light and because light is reflected from one wall to another. For example, white or near-white walls reflect light better when all the walls are white because light is reflected from one wall to another. Light reflected against a pale surface from a colored surface will give the pale surface a color casting. Gwen once had a guest room with bright red walls and an almost-white carpet. The carpet, because of reflected light from the walls, had a pink cast.
- Rooms with light-absorbing colors—dark value colors—will require more artificial light than rooms with light-reflecting colors.

Selecting a Color Scheme

The first thing to think about in selecting a color scheme is your own and your family's personality and lifestyle. What colors do you really like? What colors wear well for the people in your home? The Janssen family likes blue, and throughout the house, blue is a unifying color.

It's wise to avoid "trendy" colors, such as the chartreuse and orange of the retro craze. If chartreuse and orange express your personality, go ahead and use them, but just know that they don't wear well and the craze will probably be pushed out of the way by something else, leaving you with out-of-date colors in your home.

Base your color choices on rugs, pieces of furniture, or paintings that have an enduring quality. Both of us have used Oriental rugs as a starting place for our living room decorating. Or simply choose something in your house that you love and start your color selections there.

Don't be afraid to mix colors and prints. Just keep them in the same family. Use a sample board with all the colors, prints, and solids displayed. Live with it a while before you begin decorating the room, and then proceed with boldness.

Color My Floor

Never underestimate the significance of floors in your decorating scheme. As with walls, remember what light and dark colors do to a room. A light floor will cheer up a room and make it seem bigger. A dark floor darkens the whole room and makes it seem cozy.

While you may want to choose wall-to-wall carpeting in a neutral color, there is nothing to keep you from putting down a brilliantly colored area rug. But area rugs are not the only way to bring color to floors. You can stencil designs and paint right on the surface of wood floors. You, as did the early settlers in this country, can paint floor canvases in a big checkerboard, geometric, floral, or even a whimsical folk art design. Black-and-white checkerboard painted floors suit both traditional and contemporary decors and have been prized for many years because of their attractive versatility.

You can paint a floor to look like a marble mosaic tile. You can paint a trompe l'oeil "rug" right on the floor. You can add interest to staircases by painting or stenciling designs on the risers. Paint hopscotch or shuffleboard games on the floors of children's or recreation rooms.

Once, on a tour of very expensive homes, Gwen saw a floor in a recreation room that had large pieces of paper torn from brown paper sacks—without grocery store advertising—glued to the concrete floor, and then covered with many, many layers of clear floor varnish. The effect was a floor that looked like flagstones.

Area rugs can be changed seasonally to give the room a fresh look. Use rich colors in fall and winter. Replace them with light-colored or sisal rugs in spring and summer. Make a rag rug, or watch consignment and closeouts for great deals on area rugs. When deciding on a rug, make sure it is not too small for the space or it will look dinky. On the other hand, if it is too big, with the furniture covering much of it, the impact will be lost.

Many of us spend some time living in apartments. That means the floor color has been determined for you. While you might want to find an apartment that has carpeting that will at least not fight with the colors in your furnishings, most apartment carpeting is pretty boring. Here's a great place to put down those bright area rugs.

Sometimes area rugs are the best answer for covering worn carpets until you can replace them. Jo uses a large, floral carpet in her dining room to cover her white carpet. The rug protects the carpet from spills, and the print in the rug hides occasional stains. It also complements her color scheme and adds interest to the room.

Thoughts on Saving Money

1. Wait a while before deciding exactly what colors you want. Live in your rooms and think about your decision for a few weeks or months. Conditions and circumstances, such as available light (which can vary dramatically between the seasons), available materials, things you own, things you are about to acquire, and the desired ambience, will affect your decision.

2. If the room turns out too dark, sponge or ragroll on the same color, diluted with glaze and white paint.

3. If you think the wall you painted is too pale, invest in a quart of a darker shade and sponge or rag roll it over the paler shade.

4. Instead of using many yards of expensive decorator fabrics on curtains and slipcovers, use it for small items like pillows and valances. Then use the colors from the print to paint furniture, walls, and trim. Take a small design from the fabric to design a stencil to repeat the pattern throughout the room. It will appear as if there is a lot more decorator fabric than there is. Complement the decorator fabric with less expensive fabrics in coordinating prints, stripes, and gingham checks used in large doses for the slip covers, curtains, and other large items.

5. If you are not sure you want to add a particular color to your room, purchase a yard of inexpensive fabric, or a yard of ribbon, or some construction paper, or find something you already own in that color. Leave it out in the room, perhaps draped on a chair, to see if you enjoy living with it.

Be Bold

The most important thing to remember from this chapter is to be bold about color. Bring home a rainbow in fabrics, paints, and decorative items. Color is a decorating tool that anyone can afford. It is possible to change the visual temperature of any room by changing its color. Painting a wall in a color that pleases your family is a quick way to bring freshness into your home. When introducing a color to a room, use it at least three times in that room. Try to put one wonderful color in each room of your house. Doing so will bring beauty into your life.

If you are afraid of making a mistake, then choose to err on the side of simplicity; use lots of neutrals and harmonious, soft colors that don't scream. But if you want to live life on the edge, don't be afraid to risk—especially when it comes to paint. A room painted the wrong color can quickly be repainted to correct the error. Most of us home decorators have had to repaint a room because of poor color choice at least once in our lifetime.

Besides color, another important element in your room is windows. They are the main source of natural light, they bring heat and cold into a room, and sometimes they frame a lovely view. What you do with your windows is important, so we will explore that in the next chapter.

Shoestring Tips

- Decorate in colors you love.
- Decorate in colors you look good in.
- Buy a pint of paint and try it on one section of your wall before buying lots of paint.
- If you prefer not to test paint directly on the wall, paint a white poster board and move it from wall to wall to see how light affects the colors you have chosen.
- Don't forget the ceiling when considering color.
- Draw a picture of your room, and, using crayons or markers, color it with the colors you've chosen to get an idea of how it will look.
- Good quality paints will cover better, saving you time, effort, and, in the long run, money.
- Use paint to give color to a room—it's much cheaper than fabric. Don't be afraid to paint furniture.

CHAPTER 7

Window Wonderland

*P*erhaps nothing adds beauty to a home the way window treatments can. Without them a room looks bare and cold. You can have the most beautiful wall treatment in the world, but if after dark there are great black holes where the windows are, the room is going to seem cold.

Some people like a bare, stripped-down, clean look, but even they need window treatments to keep out the sun and give privacy. A sparse decor calls for miniblinds, vertical blinds, fabric shades, or shutters. A window treatment the same color as the wall or in a neutral color will give a clean, uncluttered look.

Most of us, however, like some softness at the windows of our homes. Remember, in many rooms windows make up a large part of the walls, and the coverings we put on them make a powerful color statement. So window treatments become an important part of our decorating scheme.

But Aren't Window Coverings Expensive?

It's true, if you go to a professional window specialist, you may need a second mortgage to get draperies in place. Don't worry—we have some thoughts about how to do your windows on a shoestring budget. You are fortunate if your home came with good window treatments—curtains and drapes that are neutral and in good taste and in good shape.

You don't have to go an expensive route to have beautiful windows. Before you panic and decide to spend any money, see if you already have what you need to meet your need for window coverings. In Jo's first home, the simple solution to the drapery problem was to switch what she already had from one room to another. She put the yellow-and-white curtains from the guest room into the nursery. The white nursery draperies went to the master bedroom, and the tan ones from the master bedroom went to the newly painted, tan-colored guest room. After the curtain and draperies were washed, starched, and ironed, they looked fresh and new. Perhaps all you need to make your existing windows treatments work is to add a roll-up shade, a valance, pretty tiebacks, or some trim. The transformation of what you already have can be pretty amazing. We're going to give you lots of ideas in this chapter. But first, let's talk about choosing window treatments appropriate to your lifestyle.

Making the Best Window Treatment Choice

Window treatments can make a room look small if they take up too much space. The living room of Jo's first home had heavy, dark green draperies and layers of sheers beneath. The whole treatment extended into the room several inches and took up valuable floor space. Further, the drapes covered about two feet of wall on either side of the windows. When the draperies were closed, the room felt like a dark green cave— they overwhelmed the room. Not every room has space to spare for heavy window treatments.

Before you start shopping for window coverings, stop and think about your lifestyle. Ask yourselves these questions:

- Is your family active and into sports? If so, you probably don't want a lot of lacy curtains hung everywhere.
- Is country your style? If so, consider whether you want a rustic country look with simple tabbed curtains or shutters, or a fluffy, ruffled country look.
- Do you have any formal rooms? How can windows in those rooms be handled inexpensively?
- Do you want to see the view from a window?

- Do you need privacy?
- Do you need protection from the light or heat of the sun?
- Are the windows drafty?
- Will you be opening this window?
- Do you have kids or pets? If so, you may want something that's out of reach for them.
- Do you need something washable? (Jo wishes the first panel of the vertical blinds covering her patio door was washable. It's gotten a little brownish where her children's hands have touched it going in and out.)
- How much light do you want to come in?
- Do you want your window treatments to be fussy, elegant, rich, elaborate and puddled, or simple, straightforward, and utilitarian?
- Do you need room-darkening coverings for day sleepers or babies?
- Do you have allergies? Dust can really kick up the allergies, so you may need some kind of window treatment you can easily keep dust free.
- Are there architectural elements of the home that you need to consider, such as vents, posts, or radiators?
- How will your home look from the outside? Your windows should look consistent and uniform. One way to achieve this is to line all drapes in the same color or use the same colored miniblinds or shades. Whatever you do, your window treatments should look good from the outside too.

Before you go shopping, take a look at some decorating magazines that emphasize the style of your home. See what kinds of window treatments are being used and what strongly appeals to you. Take a notebook and pen along when you do your research. Tear out the pages to take along when you go shopping, or draw some simple line drawings to help you remember what you like.

If your plan includes drapes, write down descriptions of fabrics (sometimes stores will give you little swatches), price per yard, or price per unit if you are planning to buy ready-made curtains and drapes along with style numbers and other pertinent information.

A walk through the drapery department of any large retail store can be an eye-opening, idea-expanding venture for the shopper. You don't have to buy the expensive draperies you see; just copy the ideas! In your notebook, sketch the idea and make notes so you will be able to remember what you like.

Visit a fabric store and check out the pattern books. In the books, you will find a section of home decorating projects. There are always several window treatment ideas. Gwen used a swag and tails pattern for her living room window treatments. She didn't pay full price for the fabric; she waited until it went on sale.

Don't limit your search just to the drapery section of the fabric store. Almost any fabric can be used for window coverings: gingham checks, denim, calico prints, and awning fabric. Before you leave the store, check out the drapery hardware section. Drapery hardware has become almost more important than the draperies. Beautiful wrought-iron rods, swag hooks, and unusual tiebacks are available in every store that sells draperies. The shoestring decorator will take a careful look at drapery rod design and price and then think about how to achieve a similar effect without the expense.

After you've visited the drapery department of major stores and fabric stores, go to a couple of the large chain discount stores. You will be amazed at the variety of inexpensive window coverings you can find ready-made in their drapery departments. Even if what you see looks too cheap, you'll know what's available.

Don't pooh-pooh these discount window coverings until you give them some thought. Gwen painted her guest room walls dark green and left all the woodwork white. Then she went to a local discount store and chose green-and-white checked tab curtains. A matching lamp shade and a checked throw rug completed the decor and were the perfect complement for a mostly green quilt she had found in a thrift store. Miniblinds provide privacy in the room. The tabbed curtains hang at the sides of the windows and a valance hangs between the curtains. The cost is minimal, but the effect doesn't look cheap; it has a warm, inviting country look.

Sometimes discount store draperies look cheap because there is not enough fabric in them. They look all right on small windows, but when you stretch them out for larger windows, they look skimpy. Of course, the solution is to buy more of the curtains, but be careful, because you may be spending more than if you went some other route.

Another way to cut window treatment costs is to keep an eye on the drapery section of your favorite thrift shop. People replace curtains and draperies, and sometimes what they cast off is not all that bad. (Gwen has seen beautiful draperies but has had no more places in her home to hang them, so they've stayed in the thrift shop.) One of the most beautiful lace window treatments Gwen ever had came from a thrift shop. A good washing and a little spray starch perked up the huge panel, and when she rehung it, it looked like a decorator's dream. For thirty dollars, Gwen also bought a huge curtain that had beautiful lace at the bottom. Now who sees lace at the bottom? She knew it would be the perfect topper for her great big bay window with a view. She cut the curtain off to valance length, and when it was finished, the valance went all the way around the bay window with lots of fullness. The rest of the curtain was cut into valance lengths and edged with lace that was being cleared out of a fabric store. She got three valances out of that one curtain.

When you're in a thrift shop, check out the fabric bins as well. People buy drapery fabric with all the right intentions, and then, for some reason, they don't make the curtains or drapes, and off to the thrift shop goes the fabric. Check out other fabrics there too.

Be sure you write down your window measurements. You have to know your window measurements exactly to know if what you are looking at will work. Keep a little retractable tape measure in your purse at all times.

One more idea for saving money on ready-made draperies is to check at places that make drapes for homes. Drapery makers do make mistakes. Sometimes the finished drapes don't fit either the size of the windows or style of the home for which they were intended. All of this is sold at a huge discount, and it just might be that a pair of drapes you find here would fit in your home. We'll say it again—know your sizes, and be willing to wait for the right drapes. You *will* find them eventually!

Some Great, Inexpensive Ideas

Well, are you ready to go shopping, or would it seem easier to just leave sheets tacked over your windows? Don't lose heart. Let's explore some shoestring solutions you can make. Don't even start making excuses. Think, instead, of all the money you'll save; if you are like us, saving money is a great motivation for learning new skills. Encourage your creative side. It may take longer to learn how to make your window coverings, but the satisfaction factor will be very high when you are finished.

Roman Shades

Roman shades can look very classy and tailored. If you don't want the fussiness of draperies or curtains, they're a great solution. They also use the least amount of fabric of all draperies. Basically, a Roman shade is one window-sized piece of decorative fabric that folds up like an accordion to the top by means of pull cords. They can be lined to protect the decorative fabric and to look better from the street. For insulation, they can be lined with a product known as Warm Windows—a thick, quilt-like sandwich of fluffy, sun-reflecting material. Warm Windows comes with instructions for making Roman shades. You'll also find instructions in many library books and in patterns at the fabric stores.

You don't have to go with a heavy look. Roman shades can be made of sheer fabrics. Sheer shades filter the light, providing a romantic look. They can be made to balloon for a fussy, elegant look. Make them of canvas or awning material and you'll get a sporty look.

You can spruce up a Roman shade by adding ribbon, trim, or stenciling on the face of the shade. The possibilities are limitless, and once you realize how simple it is to make this kind of shade, you can watch for them in magazines to glean further ideas.

Lambrequins

A lambrequin is a padded, shaped window treatment that can be used as a cornice over the window or can extend all the

Illustration 7.1
Lambrequin, finished

way to the floor like an archway over the window. Lambrequins can be straight across, curved, or a combination of curves and points. They are quite impressive and can make the window a focal point in a room. Before you install one, be sure you want that much impact from your window treatment. If you use lambrequins without curtains beneath, they will be a decorative frame for your windows and can frame a beautiful view. (See illustration 7.1)

Lambrequins do not take much decorative fabric. They are mostly wood. They are not difficult to construct, but you will need a place to build them. The best place is in the room where the lambrequin will be used since they are quite awkward to move when finished. So clear out the furniture if you can, and cover the floor to protect it. Your library has books with instructions for how to construct lambrequins.

Curtains

Depending on the type of fabric, your choice of curtain rods, and the length of the curtains you choose, you can create most any kind of mood. Curtains look best if they are full. Plan to have enough panels to make them at least two times the width of the window. But fuller than that is even better. Jo likes hers two and a half times the width.

The puddled look (where curtains are four to six inches too long and "puddle" on the floor) is popular right now. This gives a rich look, but the curtains are hard to keep clean and if you have pets and small children, they can be a disaster.

To create a look of higher windows, hang the curtains almost to the ceiling. To create an elegant look, use long curtains that reach the floor. In bedrooms and in the kitchen, stop the curtains at the sill of the window or extend them only to the bottom of the sill, to keep them out of the way.

Curtains are easy to make and can be very beautiful. Gwen had a country home with twenty-one windows. Every window had a Duette shade (a honeycomb, pleated shade) on it for warmth and privacy, and then Gwen made and hung lace curtains with a rose pattern over every window. In the winter, the curtains covered the windows. In the summer, she pushed them back to reveal the real roses that were growing everywhere outside the house. It was charming, and because she made the curtains, they were relatively inexpensive.

Lace

Lace can be used in a cute, country-style valance in your kitchen or as a layer of easy elegance in your living room. It can be used under heavier drapes or curtains or alone with shades as Gwen used hers. Remember, however, that lace does not insulate from either the cold or the sun. Depending on the pattern of the lace, it can add some privacy or almost none.

You can buy lace fabric in bolts at fabric stores—they have a wide selection. The whole resurgence of Victorian elegance has given us lots of choices when it comes to lace. In the fabric store, you will find lace panels designed to be used as café curtains or valances, along with a huge variety of lace panels designed to go under heavier curtains. You can use crocheted tablecloths or bedspreads—although, unless you inherit Grandma's, you will find that they are very expensive, even in thrift stores.

A big piece of lace can be used as a valance or gathered to cover a window in a door that has glass or in sidelights near a door. Just remember, though, that lace will deteriorate in the sun. Think about that when you hang an heirloom over the windows.

Shades

We used to think of shades as inexpensive window coverings, but no more. High quality pull-down shades can cost up to a hundred dollars each, and it doesn't pay to get cheap ones. They can tear almost before they are hung.

When visiting a store that stocks blinds and shades, you will find three different types of shades. There are the thin kinds that don't block much light or insulate, but do provide privacy. A slightly thicker shade does a better job blocking sun and insulating. Then there are the heavy-duty kind that block all light, and some even have a layer of insulative material on the back. We like this last kind, even though they are a little more expensive. In the long run, you will get more for your money.

Shades usually come in plain white or off white. If this is too plain or boring, you can stencil them or add trim, ribbon, or lace. Any combination of materials can dress up a plain Jane shade. To attach fabric, use fusible webbing or a spray adhesive. If you use a shade with sheers or lace or frame a window with curtains at the sides and lace in the middle, you can have the prettiness of the fabric treatment, plus the benefit of the shades.

There are other kinds of shades—pleated fabric shades—that, while expensive, are more durable and easier to raise and lower than Roman shades. Shades alone on the windows are rather stark and need something to soften the look. So they are used primarily under curtains, drapes, or valances.

Shutters

Shutters don't rot, fade, or grow old-fashioned. They are classic window coverings for a country or traditional decor. However, they are expensive unless you can find them on sale, in a thrift shop, or at garage sales. To make them fit, shutters can be trimmed up to an inch on top and bottom, and a half-inch or so on the sides. Gwen once bought, stained, and hung enough shutters to cover an eight-by-ten-foot window that faced the street. She bought standard stock shutters a few at a time, brought them home and stained them, and got them ready to hang. Eventually she had enough to do the whole window. Then she measured, trimmed, installed hardware, and had a permanent solution to her privacy problem.

If fitting shutters seems like too much trouble, don't worry. Find shutters as close to your window size as possible, then leave them slightly open. No one will ever know they don't fit, and they look great.

Another quick and easy idea is to put a long shutter on either side of the window. They make a lovely look. You can screw them right to the wall studs with long screws.

If you are going to paint your own shutters, we suggest you get a power sprayer to do the job. Take them outside on a windless day and spray paint them with several light coats of paint. Too much paint at one time will cause the louvers to stick and you will be unable to move them. As the shutters dry, move the louvers up and down to keep them working.

Blinds

Blinds—aluminum, wooden, mini, standard, and extra wide—are still very popular. We say "still," because Venetian blinds were used in elegant colonial homes and in the homes of the wealthy in Europe. Blinds can also be hung vertically. The latest trend is wide-slatted wooden blinds. (Vinyl miniblinds were very popular for a while, but it has recently been discovered the material emits poisonous gases. The slats also seem quite flimsy and break easily.)

If your windows are standard sizes, you can purchase mini- or vertical blinds off of the shelf at home improvement stores. Watch for sales, or do what Gwen recently did. She had two big windows that faced south, and both summer and winter sun poured in, fading everything it touched. At a thrift store, she found good aluminum miniblinds that were just a little too wide for the windows. Since they only cost five dollars each, she thought she would see what she could do with them.

Using a hacksaw she cut the top and bottom rails on both ends to shorten them. (There were some removable end clips that she took out before she cut and put back when she finished.) Then with ordinary scissors she cut all the slats all the way up the blind. When she hung them, no one could tell that they only cost five dollars each.

Metal blinds do not insulate very well; in fact, metal is a great conductor of both heat and cold. Ready-made blinds are often too long. To shorten blinds, remove the stoppers on the bottom rail and remove the string from it. Remove the desired number of slats and cut off excess string. Put it all back together. Keep the extra slats in case you ever need them to repair a bent slat. (Most blinds come with instructions for shortening the length.)

Blinds look good behind pretty curtains and function much like shades. If you pair blinds with a topper they work well in kids' room, dens, and family rooms. In kitchens and casual eating areas, blinds clean up well when there are food splatters. Blinds can be adjusted to let in light or fresh air.

If you tire of the color of your blinds, they can be spray painted. Just hang the opened blinds from a tree or clothesline outside. Choose a paint that will adhere to metal surfaces, and spray the blinds with a couple of thin coats of paint. Make sure you cover all surfaces.

Check all your usual shoestring sources for inexpensive blinds. Call places that provide special-order blinds and ask if they have any that were ordered but never picked up. You might find a deal! Of course, you can always go the route of calling a professional company and ordering blinds. They will come out, measure, order, and install the blinds. This is not an inexpensive way to go, but if there are mistakes, the company will have to make them right.

Toppers or Valances

If you determine that your blinds, shades, or other window coverings need a little softening, a topper may be the answer. Toppers are fun, because there are so many of them out there, and they are inexpensive to make.

Picture this for a little girl's room: stencil the bedspread, shams, pillows, dust ruffle, and chair pad all with the same rose bouquet design. Now add a topper with the same design over white miniblinds or shades. You could also hang silk ivy across the topper and catch it up with silk roses or rosebuds. Or add tassels, ribbon, or other decorative items to the topper.

Even windows for which privacy is not a factor may look cold and need a little dressing up. A topper of lace or decorator fabric can add a nice touch. Be sure that no matter what you put up for a topper, the fabric, color, or design is repeated in at least two other places in the room to give the room unity.

To keep proportions right, a topper or valance should measure in length no more than one-sixth the total window length.

What to Use for Curtain Rods

Most anything long and skinny enough can be made into a curtain rod. A wooden dowel can be painted or covered with fabric or wallpaper. Use copper pipe. Cover PVC pipes with fabric. Use golf clubs, baseball bats, or branches from your tree pruning. A paddle, an iron pipe, a spear, or a pole for vaulting can be used. (See illustrations 7.2)

Illustration 7.2
Paddle used as a rod

Instead of buying fancy finials for the ends of the rods, think of what else you might use. Wooden spoons or stuffed gardening gloves might work. Puncture balls of any size and kind—baseballs, tennis balls, etc.—and insert them over the ends of the rods. Use cookie cutters or wooden shapes that are available at craft stores, or form thick wire into the shape of your choice. Wire comes in silver and copper, or if you want black you can even use a coat hanger. Small ceramic figurines, Christmas tree ornaments, starfish, sea shells, artificial birds from the craft store, old doorknobs, painted or stained wooden rings, and wooden spools all will work. Use something that reflects your home and your family's taste. (See illustration 7.3.)

Illustration 7.3
Creative finials

You may have to do some creative thinking about how to attach your fanciful finials. Just remember that in some cases you have to insert the rod through the curtain or drape pocket, so you might want to attach the finials after you have done that.

Tiebacks

Here is another place to get creative. Use ropes, bandannas, western-styled belts, or bolo ties for a cowboy or southwestern theme. Use a vine of silk flowers or ivy or silk scarves for a romantic theme. Traditional cords with tassels can often be found in the usual shoestring locations. Use a wide band of the drapery fabric or a contrasting fabric used elsewhere in the room. Use big bows, gold chains with medallions, little straw hats strung together and decorated with ribbons, flowers, and bows. Use a string of large beads, a feather boa, or small wreaths. You could even braid together twigs from your garden.

Gwen once used small wreaths—each about six inches across—that cost a quarter each. She hot-glued tiny flowers on them and then attached an artificial bird. These she used in place of tiebacks. (See illustration 7.4 for other tieback ideas.)

There you have it. Dozens of ideas about window treatments, and we've only begun. We hope that we have stimulated your creative thinking about your own windows. Magazines are full of more ideas, and you will be amazed at what can be used for window coverings. Just remember, there is a way to have beautiful, fun, or charming window treatments without going broke.

Illustration 7.4
Creative tiebacks

Shoestring Tips

- Bedsheets are a great source of big pieces of yardage for curtains.
- Trim ready-made curtains with bands of ribbon, fringes, buttons, rickrack, lace, or any other trim that matches your home.
- Tab curtains are popular now and can be purchased fairly inexpensively.
- Add ribbon to the sides of the tabs, and wider ribbon along the edges of the curtains. Then add big buttons on the top edges of the curtains just where each tab ends to make them look like they are buttoned onto the rod.
- Stencil borders, motifs, or designs with fabric paints.
- Paint an outdoor scene on shades.
- Tea towels, scarves, handkerchiefs, placemats, towels, napkins, or tablecloths can be fashioned into curtains or valances.
- Old curtains can be recycled into valances.
- For new colors, consider dyeing what you have.
- Top a window with a spray of twigs, vines, or silk flowers.
- Grow a vine plant up the sides and over the top of a window.

CHAPTER 8

Frosting the Cake

Your home may have the same tan carpet, beige furniture, white drapes, and white walls as every other home on your block and still be a distinctive, beautiful home. How? With the careful and creative use of accessories and decorative details.

After your family selects a style, colors, and themes, you can then create the look you want with accessory items. It is the art on your walls, collections on display, unusual pillows and lamps, and the unique accessories you have that bring personality and designer touches to your home. By first figuring out exactly what look you aim to achieve, you can save money, because you won't bring home something that is totally unrelated to the room you are trying to decorate.

There are a lot of attractive decorative items out there, but not all of them will look good in your home. You must be discriminating. Start accessorizing your room by clearing out all of the decorative items now in the room. Only put back those objects that really fit and are of good quality. It is better to have blank spaces or too few things in a room than to have too many. Clutter isn't chic.

A word about quality: Some things just look cheap. On Jo's list of things that look cheap are pictures with fake matting, plastic picture frames, sparsely decorated straw wreaths, small "slice" rugs (shaped like a slice of citrus fruit) in kitchens, fake anything, plastic wood, polyester fur, plastic flowers, vinyl lace, and fake leather. Gwen agrees 100 percent.

One exception is silk flower arrangements. If the flowers look exactly like real flowers, there are lots of flowers in the arrangement, and they are well arranged, the result can be beautiful. Sometimes silk flower arrangements are the only solution for a dark hallway or even for a sunny area of the house. Just don't leave the same arrangement out and in the same place for years on end. (You can tear apart arrangements that have some good silk flowers and plants and reuse them in your new arrangements.)

By now you should be convinced that excellent quality goods are available at shoestring places. You'll find them if you keep your eyes open and have patience. You don't have to settle for imitation. By using real wood, real lace, real or silk flowers, and real leather, you will bring a look of richness and quality to a room. The real McCoy not only looks better but it holds up better, and if you ever want to sell it, its resale value is higher. You may pay a bit more at a thrift shop for a real wood table than a plastic table, but real wood can be refinished, while plastic surfaces cannot be. A laminated tabletop is hopeless, because when it is worn, it must be completely replaced. Leather, properly cared for, will last for generations, while its fake counterpart will soon crack and tear. That is why it is better to have a few quality items than a lot of cheap-looking stuff.

The Impact of Volume

A common mistake is to put a small decorative item or small piece of furniture in a room and let it stand by itself. It looks lonely and disconnected. It needs to be grouped with several other things to make an impact. Large-scale items can stand on their own without being grouped, or they can be the center of a grouping. Big things are easier to display and may be cheaper to obtain than the many little things required to gain the same impact. For example, a single, large, horizontal art piece over your sofa makes a bigger impact than a collection of small pieces grouped together. If you only have small objects, decide that you will get a bigger piece when possible. The bigger principle works for other decorative objects as well. One big plant placed in a corner looks less cluttered and fussy than a bunch of small plants.

Use generous amounts of fabric on a table or at the windows for a rich look. Lots of less expensive fabric over the windows looks better than a little tiny bit of expensive fabric. Stingy looks cheap. If you do not have what you want at the moment, make up your mind to wait, even if it takes a long time to get the right look. Do it right the first time, and you will be more satisfied for a long time. A few big pillows also look better than lots of small ones, but keep them in scale to your sofas and chairs. Using big things will fill a room better, require fewer items, and provide a quality look.

Displaying Collections

If you own a collection that you are proud of, it is important to display it where it can be seen and enjoyed. A few things scattered throughout a room or home has no impact. Group collectibles together, and treat them like one big item. A minimum of three things comprises a collection. An odd number of objects together—three, five, seven—look best.

You will want to display your collection in such way that shows it off and keeps it safe. Priceless or irreplaceable items should be protected under glass, in a cabinet, or in a glass case made for the collection. Don't crowd the pieces too closely. You want each individual piece to be seen.

Any surface can be used for display—walls, china cabinets, dressers, window sills, floor corners, countertops, mantels, hearths, a shelf placed over a window or about a foot below the ceiling, at the base of a large plant, on the moss around the trunk of a ficus or palm tree, on top of kitchen cabinets, or almost anywhere else!

Consider children, pets, sunlight or other available light, and traffic when choosing a place for your collection. Jo would like to put her china saucer collection on shelves on an empty wall near her back door. The wall looks plain and her collection would look nice there. But family members often slam the door, so her china would probably end up on the floor. Kids can't be expected to be careful when closing a door just to protect a precious collection. Someday she will find the perfect place for it.

Gwen's red-and-white china is in an antique hutch where it is safe. She has arranged plates to stand along the inside walls of the hutch so they can be seen. She's chosen larger pieces to display on the shelves in front of the plates. She leaves the cupboard doors standing open for a lovely display of this collection of English pottery.

Things You Can Collect

You probably have a hobby or interest that has spawned a collection. If not, let us tell you that collecting things is fun and interesting, and shoestring shopping can really feed the collecting bug because you can often find inexpensive items to add to your collection. So what should you collect? Well, what catches your eye? What interests you? What is your passion? Jo was collecting pretty china teacups for sixteen years before she realized what she was doing. Family and friends had given them to her over the years, and she had displayed them one at a time. But that didn't make much of an impact. Now she displays all of her teacups together on a shelf in her kitchen, where they can also be used for tea drinking.

You can collect any kind of household item. Spending a dollar here and a dollar there over the years makes collecting pretty painless. Collect African violets, cups, saucers, plates, pitchers, garden tools, old kitchen utensils with a colored handle, books, doorknobs, silver napkin rings, thimbles, vases,

teapots, dolls, spoons, sports team banners, inkwells, buttons, buckles, doilies, hankies, ceramic animals, cameras, doorstops, bells, something to do with your trade or hobby, bottle stoppers, piggy banks, quilts, or mirrors. The possibilities are endless!

Gwen displays a collection of interesting baskets on top of a hutch. Several wooden bowls are on another shelf. She also loves little pitchers and has a number of them hanging from pegs in her kitchen. Jo is collecting orphan china saucers because she is attracted to the pretty flowers painted on them and the fragile nature of the saucers.

Gwen started collecting black-and-white china dogs and giving them to her son as gifts. The collection has grown and has actually become quite valuable over the years.

You can find books in the library about different kinds of collectibles that can better inform you about their worth, what to look for, and where to find them. You will be surprised that objects that were commonplace a few years ago have now become collectible—like kids' metal lunch boxes. In addition to finding things to collect or add to your collection at the usual shoestring places and antique stores, if friends and families know what you collect, it will make gift giving easier for them!

"I Don't Collect Things"

You almost certainly are a collector; you just don't know it yet. Just look around your house. We are pretty sure you'll find a number of similar objects to begin your collection. Gather every little knickknack, art object, and picture from around the house. Look in the cupboards and closets and see what goes together. Remember, if you only have three things that have the same theme, you have a collection. A ceramic frog, a picture of a frog, and a book about frogs is a collection. If you have three things that are the same color, they may be the beginning of a collection. A green lamp, a green vase, and a green plate might look great together. Three things made of the same material may be just what you need for a vignette. Try a wooden box, a wooden shoe, and a wooden clock together. You may own three things that have the same function such as a wooden doorstop, an iron doorstop, and a ceramic one.

Those things that don't go with anything else can be stored until you collect other pieces, or you can give them away. Gwen often buys pretty pieces of china that she likes, even if they are orphans, and enjoys them for a time; then she might give a piece to a visiting guest who admires it or as birthday gifts to friends and nieces. Since she loves the piece so much, it is like giving part of herself.

A vignette is a nice way to display things that are not a collection, but have a common theme and look nice together. Usually a vignette includes a surface like a table, a few small items on the table—a few books, candles, a box or basket, flowers, objects d'art, a lamp—and a piece of framed art placed closely above it all. A chair, large plant, or art object nearby on the floor complete the vignette. (See illustration 8.1.)

Framing Pictures

Pictures hung on a wall need to be properly matted and framed. Visit some art galleries and other places where fine art is sold or displayed to teach your eye what looks good. You will notice that oils never have glass and mats—just ornate frames. Watercolors and prints look best under glass, singly or doubly matted, with a shallow, simple frame. You can buy art already matted and framed for you. Prints framed with cheap frames

and surrounded with fake matting will always look tacky. Save your money for the real thing.

It's tough for shoestring decorators to save money when framing pictures. You can spend hundreds of dollars on fancy framing and matting. Even if you use one of those frame-it-your-self-and-save places, the bill can really add up. Even framing that's on sale is still expensive. Try to use the simplest frame and matting you can to cut down on cost. After all, you want to see the picture, not the frame. The good news is that a properly framed and matted picture will not have to be redone for many years.

We have found some lovely art and frames at all the usual shoestring places. Gwen has a number of oil paintings for which she paid less than ten dollars each. She also has a couple of original watercolors, one of which had a good frame but a hideous matting. A new mat made it looked like a museum piece. Or find a framed and matted picture the same size as the art you want to frame. (Keep the dimensions listed in your notebook for easy reference.) Throw out the picture and use the frame, or give the picture back to the thrift shop. Jo is collecting gilt frames and simple mats at thrift stores. As she finds them, she combines them with pictures of angels she has collected. When pictures, mats, and frames come out even, she will have a collection of framed and matted angel pictures for her daughter's room.

Photos

One shoestring idea for adding fine art to your home is the use of enlarged photos. Properly framed and matted, photos look great. It is best to group either all black-and-whites or all color photos together. A current popular look is a photo surrounded with a lot of matting in a simple frame. For example,

Illustration 8.1
Grouping with collections

frame a three-by-five-inch picture in an eight-by-ten-inch frame with a mat that fills the space in between. A wall grouping with several of these looks great. The grouping will look better if the photos have a common subject matter: candid shots of your kids, a series of waterfalls, a collection of house pictures or flowers.

Gwen collected a lot of frames in white, navy blue, and silver, and put casual pictures of family members in them. They are on two bedside tables where she can enjoy them every day. You can do the same; start watching for frames of a similar look.

Another great idea for pictures is to put molding all along a wall at two different levels. Set photos on the molding and lean them against the wall. The molding needs a lip (or it could be grooved) to keep the pictures from slipping off. It is very simple to change your picture display with this kind of arrangement.

Things to Frame

If you are short on art, there are many things you can frame to create an interesting effect. You might try framing important letters, interesting envelopes (or uninteresting envelopes with interesting stamps), postcards, greeting cards, mirrors, doilies, handkerchiefs, book covers, posters, fabrics, flowers, lace bits, flowers and leaves you have pressed, and your kids' art projects.

What you can do with paint and a castoff

With today's variety of paints you can paint anything. In recent years, craft stores introduced paint that can be painted on glass and not wash off. Paints are now available that can be applied to fabric and not wash out. There is also a paint additive that will make acrylic craft paint adhere to fabric. But that's only the beginning. There are paints that look like natural materials—stone, granite, marble, and wood. They can be applied to walls, tiles, or wood with amazing results. By the time this book is in your hands, there will probably be even more special paints available to produce even more special finishes. The possibilities for what you can do with a little paint and your imagination are almost endless.

Perhaps you have an ugly orange lamp. Go to your local craft store and choose a new finish and color. Follow the instructions on the paint container, and in a few easy steps, you'll have a lamp that will look new and will also match your decor.

Not only are lamps revived with paint, other things can have new life breathed into them (or painted onto them). These may include shelves, picture frames, small tables, footstools, any furniture, vases, candlesticks, baskets, big bowls for displaying things, hat boxes, chests, clay pots, planters—you name it! After applying a finish, add stenciling or decoupage or freehand art, and your decorative item will be unique.

Oh, Those White Walls and Beige Sofas!

At the beginning of this chapter we mentioned a room with unremarkable white walls and beige furniture. Let's play with it a bit and see if we can't give that nondescript living or family room personality and style. Let's begin with white drapes, white walls, white ginger jar lamps, unremarkable side tables, and a sofa in a plain neutral or solid color that we will refer to as "sofa color." You know, just like thousands of apartments in this country filled with rented furniture. Let's see what that room would look like in traditional, country, and contemporary styles.

Traditional

Let's pretend you are the proud owner of a large blue-and-white vase that you want to display prominently in this room. You've just defined your color scheme—blue and white. We may have to spend just a *little* money because you will need fabric to create a special, traditional look. Buy some blue-and-white fabric that you like, a couple yards of blue braid, a few yards of wide blue ribbon, a fringed bedspread, and a few skeins of blue-and-white embroidery floss to make tassels. Look for the fringed bedspread in a thrift shop. You're buying it for the fringe so it doesn't matter if the spread itself is worn out. If you can't find a bedspread and don't want to wait for one to show up, you might have to buy some fringe. The fabric is the only item on the list that might be expensive. (You may also require some paint to do some stenciling and painting. It's inexpensive too.)

Look for a blue-and-white print or striped fabric. You could, however, stencil a design on plain white fabric or cut sponges in shapes and stamp on blue designs. Heavy or shiny fabrics work best for the traditional look, but use what you can find that is within your budget.

Let's say you have found (or created) a blue paisley design on a white background. We will use that paisley motif and the blue color throughout the room. To start your transformation, drape the paisley fabric over the top of the draperies. Create the fullness and shape you desire, but don't cut anything yet. Take the fabric down and measure to see how much fabric you need to create a simple swag. Now remove the fringe from the bedspread you found. Attach it to the lower edge of the swag by sewing it on, or you can even glue it in place with hot glue. Replace the swag on the top of the drapes. Congratulations—

you've just created a traditional window! If the draperies belong to you and not to a landlord, sew or glue a wide blue ribbon border down the edges of the drapes, leaving one-inch of white fabric at the outside edges. Or perhaps you'd rather use fabric paint to stencil on this border.

Now let's liven up those plain white sofas or chairs in our pretend room. Use that same blue and white print fabric and more of the fringe to make covers for your pillows. Sofas usually come with matching pillows—in this case white. Add some blue braid around the edges of those pillows and stitch tassels to the corners.

Use the rest of your blue-and-white print for a skirt on one of the side tables. Let it puddle on the floor or hem it to floor length. Spread a small, white scarf or tablecloth on top of the blue-and-white skirt. You could add some ribbon or braid to the hem edge of the white table topper to coordinate with the draperies. Add tassels to the cloth's four corners.

Next, create a stencil using a small paisley design. Stencil small blue paisleys on the lamp shades. If you still have some braid left, glue it to the lower and upper edges of the lamp shade. Another simple idea for your lamp is to sew up a paisley skirt for your lamp shade. Use a straight length of fabric that is double the circumference of the shade at its widest point. Gather the "skirt" at one edge. Slip it over the lamp shade and glue braid to the gathered "waist" of the lamp shade.

Traditional rooms need plants and flowers. Find something to use for a flowerpot or a vase. Paint it white and add blue stripes. Put flowers or plants in your pot or vase, and place your floral creation on the middle of the coffee table.

We started out with a prized blue-and-white vase. Now that you have the perfect setting for it, place it where it will be noticed. On a small table, make a vignette by placing the vase on the table and a mirror or picture on the wall over the table. Look for other pieces that have a little bit of blue.

Look through the list of traditional accessories given in chapter 2. Do you have any of them? If not, keep looking. Many of the items can be found for very little at the usual shoestring sources. Do you have a collection appropriate for this room? Find a place to display it too.

Painted white walls can be transformed into an eye-stopping decor with paint techniques. Here are three ideas. Use blue paint to stencil a chair rail about thirty-six inches from the floor. Below the chair rail, stencil tiny blue paisleys in a regular or random pattern. For a different look, try your hand at stenciling on trim that looks like wall panels all around the room at even intervals. Stencil some trim along the ceiling also. Even though this is just painted on, it will add traditional architectural detailing. A third type of paint application will cover most of the white paint. Sponge or rag on some layers of taupe and beige paint to create textural interest.

Now stand back and take a look. Your room no longer looks like everyone else's. It is uniquely yours. The walls, drapes, and furniture look distinctively traditional.

Country

Now let's turn this same plain room into a country-styled room. If you have chosen country, it may be because you have already accumulated some country pieces. Let's pretend you have inherited the colorful quilt that once covered great-grandma's brass bed. It has many prints, but pink and red florals seem to dominate. Sounds like the beginning of a color scheme to us! Hang the quilt on the wall as a focal point, or drape it over the large sofa.

Check the cupboard to see if there are fabrics you can use. If not, you'll need to go shopping for fabrics in one or more prints that have red or pink on a background of beige or white (the sofa color). Look for flowery prints, small dots, ginghams, stripes, and checks. You might find these in tablecloths, sheets, old bedspreads, and curtains. You know by now where to shop for them! You will also need a number of yards of ruffled lace and lace yardage. Look for old curtains or tablecloths to provide what you need. Get a few yards of very wide rickrack and one-inch ribbon in pinks and reds. As usual, we will also be doing some fun things with paint.

Use some of that flowery fabric to make a deep (14- to 19-inch) gathered valance and matching tiebacks for the white curtains. An alternative is to drape a large square of fabric or a tablecloth in the right colors over the top of the curtains so a large triangle hangs down.

Use more of the print fabric to cover the pillows. Add ruffles or ruffled lace to the edges, or take those plain sofa pillows and glue or sew on pink or red rickrack around the edges. Cover the side table with more pretty printed yardage. Trim the hem with rickrack. Place a square of lace on the top.

Improve that plain white lamp by stenciling on some red and pink flowers. Add ribbon or rickrack trim to the lamp shade. Or sew a skirt for the lamp shade, and cinch the waist with a ribbon and a bow.

On the coffee table, place some country collectibles. Find three or more cheap candleholders (maybe right there in your cupboard) and paint them white, pink, or red. Add little pink stripes or dots to them. Tie a ribbon in a bow near their tops, and insert tall white candles. Now you have a country collection to show off.

In a corner, place a large basket with balls of pink, red, white, and green yarn or rags that have been ripped into strips then wound into a ball. Use a real ball as a base, and you will achieve a sizable ball sooner and will use less fabric. Fill three clay pots with plants or flowers and display on a shelf or table-top. Have a flower arrangement somewhere in the room. Do you have any other country style items for this room? Create a vignette with them.

Now for the walls. The simplest idea is to paint the walls up to the chair rail with pink paint. Stencil a floral border at the chair rail. To get a little fancier, sponge on a few shades of pink or paint stripes below the stenciled chair rail border. Add another border at the ceiling. Or leave the walls white and add borders at chair-rail height and at the ceiling. To add even more country flavor, stencil a pot of ivy near the floor next to a door. Continue painting the ivy up, along, and over the doorway.

Now add your own country possessions to this cheerful room. Congratulations! You have created a welcoming place full of country charm.

Contemporary

Clear out the clutter, and we will see if we can make your ho-hum white room into a picture of contemporary sophistication. We will build the room around a large piece of modern art that has shocking red in it. We will give you two alternative color choices here: one that is monochromatic and one that uses a lot of black and white with red accents.

First, the monochromatic scheme. The room is already all white, so that is the color we will use. You will need to add some decorative items for interest. Use simply shaped white or off-white objects to make a grouping or collection. If they are big enough, they can fill a corner. Give some of your finds a white marble finish and they will have a very rich look.

Build a tall pedestal, marbleize it, and top it with a simple sculpture you have purchased or made. This will give the room some height. On the coffee table group an odd number of simple, tall, clear jars or vases. Fill each one with a red flower to bring out the red in the big piece of modern art. Cover one or two pillows with red fabric for your third use of red in your monochromatic room.

Now let's do the black-and-white room. Once again, you will need to find or acquire a few items. Look for some silver paint, shiny black fabric, shiny black paint, black braid, and one-inch wide ribbons in red and gray. The windows won't require much. We only need to add tailored tiebacks made from black fabric. Use more of the black fabric to make pillow covers. Sew red and gray ribbons on the pillows in a striped pattern. Stripes will be the motif we repeat elsewhere in the room. Paint the lamp black. Stencil or paint freestyle silver stripes on it. Trim the shade with black braid.

On the coffee table, arrange an odd number of empty glass jars. Using freehand painting or stenciling, apply silver and black stripes to them. In each jar place one red flower. Another cheap and easy way to make a contemporary collection is to paint an odd number of four-by-four-inch blocks of wood all black or all white. Use them as candleholders for large, red pillar candles.

Feel free to use the black and silver paint on items you have found. Make some of them look like black marble or gray granite. Use things with simple shapes—balls, boxes, blocks of wood, rocks, and bricks. Put them together as a collection or as part of a vignette.

The walls can be left plain white, or you can be a little more creative and add some texture. The easiest way to do that is to sponge a pale gray wash on the walls. To add architectural interest and a little richness, use a marbling technique to create faux marble trim along the ceiling, around windows and doors, and on the baseboards.

Isn't it amazing what you can do with a little fabric, paint, and creativity? And we aren't done yet! Next, we have a whole bunch more ideas for adding shoestring accessory details to your rooms.

Well, we've covered a lot of ground! We have many more helpful suggestions for each specific room of your house. But there's one more very important principle we need to cover first. It has to do with basic room arrangement and is the subject of the final chapter in this section.

Shoestring Tips

- Rotate your accessories to make your rooms feel fresh and new.
- If you have space to store them, have seasonal silk flower bouquets and bring them out for each new season.
- Learn from pros in furniture and art galleries and other places where accessories are sold. Walk around and observe how accessories are used in a room setting. It doesn't cost a thing to window-shop.
- There should be about eight and one-half inches between a table and the piece of art displayed over it.
- Give height to a room with tall pieces of furniture and large wall hangings.
- Use a large statue or ceramic animal to fill a corner.
- Two pictures of identical size should be hung one above the other.
- Three identically sized pictures can go side by side horizontally, or in a pyramid shape.
- Before hanging a picture, mark the spot with a bit of masking tape. It will show you where to put the hanger, and it will also help prevent the wall's crumbling around the hole.
- Decoupage art or photos to a room-dividing screen.

- Hang a quilt or other textile piece.
- Display a collection of wicker baskets on a kitchen wall.
- Don't be afraid to add whimsy to a room by including an unexpected "fun" knickknack or other item.
- Stencil a border around the edge of a mirror.
- Add homemade dried vines and swags of dried flowers over a bed, window, or door.
- For a really rich look, add several layers of fabrics at your windows and on your tables.
- To display a collection on a wall, first arrange it on the floor on newspaper. All the pieces collectively should form a simple shape. When you have your arrangement laid out, trace it on the newspaper that has been cut to the size of your arrangement. Tape the newspaper in place on the wall, to see how your arrangement will work.
- Add trim or braid to a pillow or lamp shade to give it a look of quality and to add detail.
- Make fabric skirts for lamp shades complete with ribbons and bows.
- Add stenciled designs to a lamp shade.
- Glue small things to a lamp shade—silk leaves, beads, pompoms, fringes, buttons, charms, feathers, fake gems, twigs, paper clips, stars, brads, fly fishing lures, pine needles, tiny bows, tiny plastic animals, pebbles, or anything small enough to stay on. Apply them in a random polka-dot pattern.

CHAPTER 9

Where Shall I Put It?

Now that you have collected some beautiful furnishings, lovely accessories, stunning art and rugs, and more, it is time to make it all look fantastic and work together for your purposes. Your rooms might not be comfortable yet, or perhaps you can't get through them without circumnavigating furniture or bumping into something. Perhaps you even have a room that is like the one Gwen once had.

It was her first home and her very first attempt at decorating. Gwen had almost no furniture of her own, but a church had loaned her a huge, three-piece, dark green sectional sofa. Of course, sectionals go together—right? So Gwen put all three pieces together on one side of the room, opposite the front door. She had also been given a huge plant and there was a corner by the sofa where it would just fit. Since the front door opened right into the living room, she put nothing on that side of the room in order to keep it free as a passageway. As she stood back to view the results, she felt as if the room were

about to tip over. That obviously didn't work. She corrected the balance by hanging a big picture on the entry side of the room, then placed a long narrow table beneath the picture. (See illustration 9.1.)

In this chapter, we want to give you some guidelines to help you make the most of what you have. You will learn how to plan a room so that all of your pieces work together and the room functions as intended. Now, don't panic and think you will need to run out and buy more furniture. Remember, this is a book about saving money. It's quite possible that you have everything you need to make your home comfortable and beautiful. Remember two of our most important rules: (1) look creatively at what you have before you buy anything, and (2) never relegate furniture to a single use. Your living room may simply need a dresser from the bedroom or a wrought-iron chair from the deck to bring balance and harmony to it.

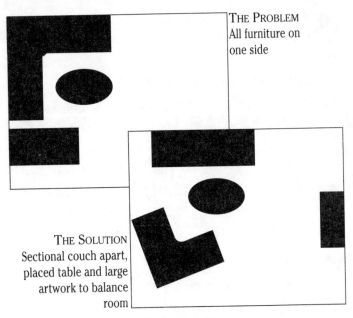

THE PROBLEM
All furniture on
one side

THE SOLUTION
Sectional couch apart,
placed table and large
artwork to balance
room

Illustration 9.1
Gwen's solution to decorating problem

Room Arrangement Basics

Before we decide where to put our furniture, let's talk about the basics of successful room arranging: traffic flow, conversation groupings, focal points, and balance.

Traffic Flow

A major consideration that many people ignore is how traffic flows through a room. Family members and guests should be able to move easily from one room to another without fear of bumping into things and without disturbing any activities occurring in the room. Have you ever been in the middle of visiting someone when a person moved from the bedroom to the kitchen for a drink of water, walking between you and your host? Or have you been watching television and realized, after a while, that it was like watching a parade because people continually passed between you and the screen? These are indications that you need to rethink the room arrangement.

Conversation Groupings

Another important element especially in a family room/den/living room is making the seating conducive to conversation. Seating must be arranged so that guests can talk without shouting, looking through a lamp, or turning completely sideways in their seats. An arrangement that allows for ease in conversation is known as a "conversation grouping," and it is a very important consideration for your guests' comfort. Seating should be close enough for easy communication, but not so close that everyone is bumping knees. About eight to nine feet at the farthest points works well. A conversation group will be arranged around a focal point, which brings us to the next point.

Focal Point

Every room needs a focal point. It should be something big to which everything in the room seems tied. In a bedroom, it will likely be the bed. In a dining room, the table is usually the focal point. In a family room or living room, it could be a rug, an entertainment center, an armoire, or a prominent painting. Some rooms have natural focal points, such as a fireplace or a picture window with a view.

Jo's living room focal point is a beautiful area rug her father-in-law brought home from Egypt many years ago. She has grouped furniture around it, and placed a glass-topped coffee table on top of it (the glass top doesn't hide the beauty of the rug). In our family rooms, both of us group all the seating around a fireplace. Also we have placed our TVs near the fireplace for easy viewing and enjoyment of both simultaneously. We have made sure there is no traffic in front of the seating area. And we both have a large coffee table in front of the seating area as a place to put books, games, magazines, coffee cups, and feet.

Balance

Another important element of room arrangement is balance. Is there a pleasing sense of symmetry? Or does the room seem to tip over like Gwen's first attempts at decorating? Is there an accent piece or a visual element that could be added to another place in the room to bring balance? Does the room seem too low? Perhaps one tall item is needed to add height.

Certain kinds of furniture can skew a room's balance. For example, lots of legged tables and chairs look, well, too leggy. Consider covering some of those leggy tables with skirts or find some furniture that is skirted to the floor.

Think about what you have that you could put in those empty corners to soften them. What about a tall display case or a large plant or a folding decorative screen?

Don't feel that you have to put every piece of furniture against a wall. It's all right to "float" furniture in the middle of the room to achieve a cozy conversation grouping or to allow for a traffic pattern. You can actually create a room within a room. Look at illustration 9.2 for a good example of this.

Windows and Lighting

Lighting throughout the room should be evenly distributed to prevent dark corners. You need to consider such things as electrical outlets where you can plug in lamps for reading. You'll also need a table, a small chest, or a hassock close at hand where you can put your reading material and a cup of coffee.

Windows let in light, views, drafts, and harmful rays that fade furniture and destroy curtains. Your favorite reading chair will not be comfortable next to a drafty window.

Now that you've thought through the way traffic will move through the room, and you've found a focal point and grouped your conversation area around it, ask yourself these questions:

1. For what other purpose, besides conversation, will the room be used? (Use the survey in appendix A to help you assess your needs.)
2. Where are the heating and air-conditioning vents, the electrical outlets, and phone jacks?
3. If you have a favorite collection, where are you going to put it?

Illustration 9.2
Good example of grouping

Don't Touch That Furniture

Most people arrange their furniture by shoving and pushing it here and there until everything fits. You can save your back and avoid a lot of stress if you first work out your furniture arrangement plan on paper. By drawing your room on a grid, you can see the placement of electrical outlets, heating and cooling vents, windows, doors, and, perhaps most importantly, you can plan your traffic patterns with a touch of a finger, rather than a shove of the furniture.

Here's how to do it. Either purchase a pad of one-fourth inch grid (graph) paper (it comes in a tablet at any store that sells office supplies, including your local supermarket or drugstore), or make your own. Use this as your scale: every one-fourth inch equals one foot.

In order to make a diagram of your room, you must carefully measure it. Transfer your measurements to the graph paper. Be sure you draw in fireplaces and other built-in architectural elements of the room, such as windows and doors. Then put in all those outlets and vents. Built-in lights, pipes, and radiators should also be indicated because they may influence where you place certain pieces of furniture.

Then measure your furniture pieces, paying attention to chairs with backs extending beyond the legs of the chair or recliners that will need more space in the front. Think about how much space a table with drop leaves will need when those leaves are extended. Remember that chairs you pull out from tables require at least three feet of open space. After you've made all your measurements, record them in your decorating notebook so the next time you want to move furniture you won't have to remeasure every piece. This probably will not be the last time you rearrange your furniture.

In the back of this book (appendix B) we have provided you with furniture shapes that have been drawn to the one-fourth-inch-equals-one-foot scale—the same as your graph paper. You can photocopy, trace over, or cut out the furniture shapes that are the sizes of your furniture.

Once again, think about traffic patterns and analyze how traffic would best flow from one room to another. These include the paths a person may take to enter and exit the room, and secondary paths to a closet or window. Pencil these traffic patterns right onto your grid.

Next think about what will be your focal point. What will be the room's best feature—the one that catches your eye when you walk into it? We've talked about this at length above, so just remember to include that focal point on your grid.

Now think about the zones of activity in the room. Identify where people are most likely to congregate to talk, eat, watch television, read, or look at a display of collectibles. Small rooms usually only have one zone. Larger rooms may have several. The number one zone of the room should always be near the room's focal point. This is also where you should place your major grouping of furniture.

Start arranging your furniture by placing the largest pieces first. These will probably be the sofa, a piano, a bed, or the dining room table. Then put in the small tables and occasional chairs. Keep moving paper pieces on the grid until you find an arrangement that doesn't place all the big pieces of furniture on one side of the room, includes a conversation grouping or two (if needed), and allows at least three to four feet in those all-important traffic areas. Coffee tables should not be closer than eighteen inches to the seating area. Viewers should not be closer than about nine feet from the TV screen, depending on the size of the screen.

Chairs can't sit alone. They need a small table or another flat surface near-by. There needs to be a lamp and perhaps a hassock or footstool. Most furniture looks best as part of a vignette, so create several groups in your room. The whole grouping will include a major piece of furniture, a mirror and/or art objects, pillows, a throw, and other decorative objects.

Try to avoid placing several tall pieces together. A grandfather clock, a tall secretary desk, and a bookcase should not be placed side by side. Put some horizontal object between them. Remember the need for balance in the room.

Challenging Situations

At this point, you may be thinking there is no way you can make your room work. Jo is frustrated by home designers who don't take real life into consideration when they design homes. Sometimes we have to use extension cords to make up for inadequate outlets. Sometimes we have to invent a divider to separate an entryway or eating area from the rest of the room. Jo confesses that she has covered a heating vent with bookcases because the family has many, many books. There was simply no other way to get all those books put away.

It's a frustrating fact that few rooms are perfect. Gwen is living in a home where the front door opens into a hallway attached to the living room. She's created an entryway with a decorative folding screen between the living room and the hallway.

Eating spaces, offices, music rooms, and craft and sewing corners can be created with a little imagination and sleight of hand. By placing a sofa, entertainment center, piano, bookshelves, or other large pieces in the right places, you can pretend you have a wall and—presto—a room is created.

Gwen wanted a room in her basement for her son to live in while he finished college. Basement remodeling is notoriously expensive, so she created a "room" by placing a ten-foot wall of bookshelves along one side of the "room" and an entertainment center at one end of the "room." The concrete foundation walls that had been sprayed with a textured plaster formed the other two walls. She purchased white sheets at a thrift shop for two dollars each and stapled them to the ceiling to cover the unfinished wood and insulation, then covered the staples with thin slats of wooden trim. It wasn't perfect, but it was inexpensive and met the need.

When you think you have a workable, pleasing arrangement of furniture—on paper—tape down the paper furniture shapes and live with your plan a while before you move the furniture physically. Having the plan on paper will also help you analyze if you need more furniture or if you need to eliminate some. It is better to have too little furniture in a room than too much. When you are ready to add a piece, take your plan to the furniture store, and make sure that the piece you are selecting will fit perfectly.

What's the Big Picture?

The placement of wall art greatly affects the appearance of a room. Art can add importance to a focal point and height and balance to a room. Have you ever seen a lonely photo or a twelve-inch wreath on a big wall, not close to anything else—just floating there alone? Or pictures spread out too much to cover more wall? Or the home of a tall friend who hangs art at her eye level, not yours? Let's look at some principles for wall decoration. (See illustrations 9.3 and 9.4.)

Illustration 9.3
Wall art no-no

Illustration 9.4
Wall art solution

Start with an empty slate by taking everything off the walls. Give your mind a clean slate too. Forget that you bought a certain picture to go above the sofa in a particular room. Take a fresh look at everything.

Pictures need to relate to something else in the room. So the pictures could be the same color as the furniture, the same motif (like checks), the same subject (like dogs), or the same theme. They need to hang above a chair, a table, another picture, or a chair rail to form an eye-pleasing group. Think of the wall art and the furniture, plus any architectural element, as a related grouping.

A picture cannot stand alone unless it is very big and important. Generally, it is better to put groups of pictures on a wall and leave lots of empty wall space around them. Pictures in a grouping don't need much space between them. Set them as close together as looks good when you stand back and view the whole grouping.

Pictures hung together as collections should have a common subject, color, theme, or similar frames. Try to integrate other objects in the room into the arrangement. As we've already mentioned, Gwen has an English hunt theme in her living room. Over a game table, which contains a tall lamp, Gwen has hung small hunt scene pictures on either side of the lamp and a small English transfer ware plate with horses and a carriage scene. All of these small pieces work together to make an attractive arrangement that includes the necessary lamp.

Your art arrangement will work best if you preplan it before you pound nails in the walls. Here's how you do it:

1. Measure the space where the pictures will be hung. Then mark out the measurements on the floor, using newspaper as a template.

2. Arrange the pictures on the newspapers. Balance two or three smaller pictures against one large one. Move them around until you like the appearance of the arrangement. The largest picture in a group should be in the middle.

3. If you are hanging three pictures in a row, make sure the spacing between them is consistent.

4. Pull up the hanging wire on the back of each picture. Measure from the taut wire to the center top of the frame. Be sure to include this measurement when determining the distance of a picture from the ceiling.

5. Transfer your arrangement measurement to the wall with light pencil marks. Or trace around each picture on the newspaper, cut out the shapes, and tape them to the wall. Then step back and view the arrangement.

6. Position your picture hooks and hang your pictures. Check that the pictures are hanging straight. The overall shape of the finished grouping should be symmetrical, but it doesn't need to be square. It could be a rectangle, oval, triangle, or inverted triangle. A sofa grouping could be in an L shape, extending lower on one side of the sofa. (See illustration 9.5 for ideas.)

Place the piece with the most visual weight—usually, but not always, the biggest piece—in the center of what will be your arrangement. Then work other pieces into your arrangement to form the shape you have in mind. Don't be discouraged if it doesn't work the first time. You may need time to think about an eventual addition to your arrangement to make it work. Or some pieces may have to be eliminated to achieve balance.

Place pictures as close as possible to the object to which you want them to relate. Remember: A piece of wall art should be hung no more than eight and one-half inches above a sofa, table, or other thing it's relating to. For example: Place a chair

Illustration 9.5
Ideas for wall art groupings

with floral upholstery next to a table with a flower arrangement on it. Then hang a picture of flowers above the furniture grouping for a pleasing arrangement of related items. Jo has two wonderful, old Japanese prints that she has placed on either side of a china cabinet about eight and one-half inches above the chair rail. Both the cabinet and pictures have bamboo frames.

Think not only of the shape of the picture group, but consider what the furniture around it adds to the shape. A sofa under a grouping that includes a large picture in the center and several smaller ones will create a triangle shape, a shape that is pleasing to the eye. Jo's china cabinet with the two Japanese prints on either side forms a cross, another pleasant shape.

Another nice way to effectively display art is to put it between two large architectural items like two doors, a door and a window, or two big windows. If you are using only one picture, it must be big enough to fill the space nicely.

Show It Off

Similar rules apply for accessories and collections. A group of small items that are somehow related should all be put closely together for more impact. This works for tabletop collections as well as wall art. For example, suppose you collect ceramic dogs. Group several of them closely together at the base of a lamp, then hang a small picture of a dog near the lamp as part of the grouping.

A tabletop isn't the only place to display collections:

- Hang plates in a circle-shaped grouping above a table.
- Group angel figurines together at either end of a mantel.
- Place groups of interesting candlesticks on either side of a hearth.
- Fill a shadow box with miniature objects.
- Put a shelf above a door and fill it with birdhouses.
- Fill a shelf with a teapot collection.
- Stack a collection of wooden boxes under a sofa table.
- Fill one shelf in a bookcase with antique piggy banks.
- Place a collection of umbrellas or canes with interesting handles in an umbrella stand.
- Open a cupboard door to display a collection of quilts.
- Display teacups in a wall shelf, a case, or a cupboard.
- Use a window shelf to show off bottles.
- Stack antique lunch pails or bread boxes on top of a refrigerator.
- Place water pitchers on a soffit in the breakfast area.
- Group dolls in a little-used chair in a corner.
- Group candles, figurines, books, and other objects on a mantel.

Your collections say something about you. They should be on display for everyone to enjoy. Just remember the rule of three: *Three things placed close together always look complete.* An odd number of things grouped together looks better than an even number.

Finding Storage Space

There is no such thing as a house with too much storage. You can, however, get more storage by choosing furniture with drawers and shelves so that they do double duty as storage pieces. A chairside table is fine as a place to put a lamp, a book, and a cup of coffee. But a chairside piece that has shelves or drawers not only serves as a place to set your reading material, but as a storage place for games, craft projects, magazines, and other items you want handy. There are many double-duty pieces on the market. We have seen headboards, beds, coffee tables, dining nook sets, benches, hassocks, butcher block carts, and bedside tables that have storage space.

Gwen found one of her favorite double-duty pieces in a thrift shop. It is a solid maple school desk, complete with a pencil groove on the top and a nice deep shelf under the top. The desk makes a great side table because books and magazines can be slipped onto the shelf when the reader has finished for the evening.

Chests are wonderful double-duty pieces. Jo has a wicker one beside the living room couch. She has another one she uses as a footrest in front of her favorite chair in the bedroom. Gwen padded the top of her cedar chest and used it as a telephone bench for many years. Then she tore the padding off and used it as a place to put a television set in a bedroom. She also has a round top trunk she picked up in a thrift shop where she puts extra blankets and also the pillows for the outdoor furniture.

Jo's daughter sleeps in a captain's bed, and her toys are stored in the drawers under the sleeping platform. It can work for adults to have a platform bed too. Jo has also used good, sturdy wooden boxes—which you can either purchase or build—in front of a window to form a window seat storage area. Those same sturdy boxes built with slots can hold your shoes beneath the seat and be put in a walk-in closet to sit on when changing shoes.

Beautiful band or hat boxes are available everywhere and provide storage that is too pretty to put away. Stack decorative boxes under a table or on a shelf in plain view. Jo has a decorative box sitting under a dresser to hold out-of-season clothes. Stuff things under skirted tables. No one will ever know they're there. Slide large, flat storage boxes under beds.

Another way to create more storage space is to empty cupboards or closets of unwanted stuff. Look around your house for accumulations of rarely used things. Pack them up and give them away. Make it a habit to periodically throw out things that are not being used regularly. Voila! You've just discovered new space.

A good way to add storage is to use forgotten places.

- Put a shelf over a doorway. Put brackets about ten inches down from the ceiling and fasten the shelf on top. It can go all the way around the room and is great for storing books, collections, or cooking implements like big pots or tureens.
- Check behind a door. Is there room for a bookcase or extra shelves?
- Put cup hooks above a stack of china.
- Stack lift-out trays in deep drawers to form two layers for more storage. Put racks and shelves on the back of pantry and closet doors.
- Think about putting a shelf in your bathroom to hold extra towels and add pretty jars to store soaps. Or use that space over the toilet for shelves for towels, soaps, and other necessary or decorative items. Does your pedestal sink leave you with no storage space? Add a skirt and attach it with Velcro to provide a hidden space for storage under the sink.
- Hang things from the ceiling. A pot rack can be used not only for pots but also to hang small baskets to hold onions and garlic. You can also hang pot holders

and watering cans there. Anything with a handle can be hung on a pot rack.

- Hang wire baskets—the kind that have three baskets in graduated sizes. They can be used for fruit and vegetables, but they can also be used for shampoo, extra towels, and face cloths, and the big one will even hold a hair dryer.

Wardrobes, armoires, or tall cupboards are some of the most useful pieces of furniture ever created. Gwen has used one of hers (she has three) as a bookcase, a place to store fabric and sewing supplies, for clothing, and as a display cabinet for her collection of red-and-white transferware pottery. Big pieces like these also provide a focal point in a room.

Since both of our households cater to writing, reading, and other facets of the publishing business, books are a real problem—as in too many books. Jo solved her problem with floor-to-ceiling, wall-to-wall shelves. This unit is in her family room (although it isn't the only place her family stores books) and was made for her by a handyman. Put books in the dining room in bookshelves built around doorways. Put books in shelves under windows or around a breakfast nook, or turn a closet into a library.

By now you should have put aside all preconceived ideas about how certain pieces of furniture can be used. It's possible to redefine the use and place for almost everything you own.

What do you have in one room that could fill a great need in another? Think about it.

Shoestring Tips

- Do the graph exercise described in chapter 9 to decide how to better arrange your rooms.
- Remove extra items from a room.
- Decide on a focal point for your room.
- Figure out how you want traffic to move through your home.
- Create a grouping (vignette) in a room.
- Add a shelf for displaying a collection.
- Cover a box with paper, wallpaper, fabric, or contact paper for decorative storage.
- Clean out cupboards, closets, and other places where things accumulate.

CHAPTER 10

Entry and Living Room

First Impressions Are Important

The moment someone walks through your door, an impression of you and your home begins to form. It may be a positive impression: "My, how neat and clean this place is! No slobs living here." or "Mmmm. Smells good, looks good—must be good!" On the other hand, the initial reaction may not be so pleasant: "What a mess! How do people live in this?" or "This place needs a decorating overhaul." The initial introduction to your home will be the foyer or entryway and the living room. So that's where we'll begin.

The Entry

We both like to make our living rooms and entries as attractive and welcoming as possible while introducing the mood and style of our homes. Gwen's entry tells visitors that a country hunt theme awaits them in the colors red and blue. Jo's entry is separated from her living room by just a half-wall. Together the two areas let people know that the Janssens like books, gardening, and the color blue.

In some homes, there is no separate entry. People just open the front door and step directly into the living room. That abrupt feeling can be alleviated in a number of ways. You can use a folding screen to create an entryway or put up a piece of latticework. A wall hanging or plants hung from the ceiling could divide the area. Perhaps the simplest way to create that separate entry space is with creative and careful furniture arrangements.

Any large piece of furniture can act as a divider. You can use furniture to create a separate area that could be defined as an entry. Jo once strategically placed a drop-leaf table to give the impression of a separate entry in her little Salem cottage. Even something as short as a small table, desk, or sofa will do the trick.

A small, color-coordinated area rug will protect the carpet from wet and muddy shoes. You may want to remove the carpet from the area by the front door and apply a more durable flooring like wood, tile, or linoleum. This will further define the entry space and protect the carpet from soiling. A durable surface here will delay the need to replace the carpet.

With either a real or improvised entry, you may want to include some of the classic entry furnishings. It is often customary to place a mirror over a table or narrow shelf in your entry so you can check your appearance before answering the front door or going out for the day. Guests like to check their appearance, too, especially on windy days. If there is room, a table or shelf can display pretty things, and if it has a drawer this is a great place to put the car keys. Plants, a seat, a hall tree, and an umbrella stand are all typical entry furnishings. They are not required, though, so if you have no room for them, do not crowd them in. People should be able to walk safely into your home without worrying about knocking over a coat tree or tripping over a plant.

If you have no room for more than a mirror and a narrow shelf, you can pretend there is more there with a mural you stencil, paint, or wallpaper on the wall. We have seen garden scenes, shelves holding decorative objects, benches, a stone archway, a fountain, and windows with an outdoor scene showing through the "panes" and many more tromp l'oeil effects applied to the walls. Jo has stenciled two topiaries in her tight entry space to introduce her garden theme. Gwen uses a folding screen with a hunt scene painted on it to divide her entry from the living room.

A shelf for your entryway can be easily constructed by attaching brackets to the wall (be sure you find a stud to attach to) and laying something across the top. It can be a piece of thick glass with the edges smoothed, a piece of painted, pressed particleboard (you may want to glue on a decorative wood trim around the edges and attach it from beneath with short screws), or a piece of marble. (If you use marble, be sure the brackets are strong enough to hold its weight.) Wood shelves can be given a faux stone or marble finish.

The Living Room

A formal front living room, not used also as a family room, is a luxury many of us manage to live without. It is usually a showplace used for entertaining adults. Many new house plans eliminate a formal living room and use a "great" room idea instead, a more informal living space. If you have a formal living room, however, it provides a clue to the rest of your home and makes either a good or bad first impression to guests. If you do not have a "real" living room, you will still benefit from this chapter because you may want to use some of the ideas for your family room that also must function as your living room when guests arrive.

Jo dreamed for many years of having a "real" living room—a room set apart for entertaining adults and a place to show off her "fine taste" in furniture and collectibles. Oh, she would use it often, and people would be so impressed with her well-maintained room. Well, she now has a real living room, and it usually does look fairly neat and clean, but she doesn't use it nearly as often as she envisioned. Gwen has begun to reconsider the usefulness of a formal living room because hers too is almost never used. Jo's living room presents a lovely first impression for people entering her home—except when it is being used as a classroom for her daughter and her twenty-five dolls and animals. Sometimes Al, Jo's husband, goes there to read to escape the noise of the family room. And every once in a while, the Janssens actually entertain in their living room! Usually, however, they end up chatting over their cappuccinos in front of the fire in the family room. Gwen's guests usually end up hanging out in the combination kitchen-family room.

If we are typical, then the typical living room has become something like the Sunday parlor of Victorian days. Because the living room (what a misnomer that has become) receives only light use, it's a great place to safely display your fragile collections, expensive lamps, and finest furniture. This is the place for silk and linen fabrics, antiques, silver candlesticks, crystal vases, and anything we wouldn't trust around the everyday wear and tear of active family life.

This room may stay bare for a while if it is low on your priority list. You may simply not have the money to begin decorating it. That is OK. *Keep to your plan and stay within your budget.* While you are waiting, you can be gathering ideas for your room and deciding how you eventually want it to look and function. You'll have time to refinish a certain piece of furniture for the room. You'll find interesting things to go in your living room at garage sales and thrift shops. As the room gradually comes together, it will look better all the time, and you'll probably have enough time to think about each addition so you won't make decorating mistakes.

A living room requires a conversation area. The major expense will be good seating. A collection of comfy chairs works well. Some of our friends collected four wing chairs at estate sales. They didn't really match very well until they found a rug with colors from all four chairs. The chairs grouped around the rug in front of a fire is cozy and inviting.

A sofa and loveseat set is a typical solution, but it is not the only successful formula for a conversation area. That combination often doesn't fit into many living rooms. Not all living rooms will have a wall long enough to use a long sofa. Keep that in mind if frequent moves are in your foreseeable future.

Gwen has two love seats and a couple of wing chairs placed in a rectangle, which seats six people comfortably. One love seat and two or more comfy chairs may give you more flexibility. Although a long sofa may seem like a good solution for lots of seating, people don't always like to sit in a row or too close together when they visit. Remember to keep the seating in a conversation group close (nine feet or less) so people can communicate easily. Be sure there is enough space for guests to get in and out of their seats without bumping knees with those seated nearby or running into a coffee table.

There needs to be a place for the inevitable cup of coffee and a dessert plate. Most of us serve beverages, snacks, and desserts in the living room, so think through where your guests are going to set their plates and cups. Side tables or nesting tables that can be pulled out when needed are handy. A coffee table in front of a sofa will serve the people sitting on the sofa. (See the list of ideas in chapter 5, "New Ways of Looking at It," to figure out how to make a side table or a coffee table from objects you may never have considered before.)

Most modern living rooms do not have a central ceiling light, so we typically use table lamps placed evenly around the room. To make more room on your side tables, though, you can eliminate lamps and use track lighting, recessed lighting, or floor lamps instead. (Don't forget, however, to have a task light at a desk and a good reading light by your favorite reading chair.) Special lighting can highlight art and collections and will add drama and beauty to a living room. When you plan the room arrangement, strive for balance not only in furniture but also with the lighting to prevent any dark areas.

A corner of a living room may be needed to store a rarely used dining table for infrequent formal dining. We will discuss that more in the chapter about eating areas. If your dining room is part of, or connected to, your living room, you will be decorating both in such a way that they flow together.

The living room may also function as a library. Books add character to a room. A lot of smaller bookcases scattered around will only make a room seem cluttered. One large mass of bookcases covering one wall looks so much more impressive and makes arranging furniture easier. Try to have the bookcases go as high as the ceiling. Built-ins look wonderful, but you can get a built-in look by adding trim to the edges where ceiling-high bookcases meet the ceiling. Consider building cases on either side of the fireplace or on a wall with a window. If you have lots of books, a shelf can even extend above the window. A padded window seat under the window would be inviting for the bibliophile.

Alice in Wonderland, or Kids in Fragileland

In her first home, Jo had no separate family room so she made an extra bedroom into a playroom. This allowed her front living/family room to function more as a living room. She still had to keep it baby- and toddler-proof though. If you have children around often, consider their needs when decorating your living room. Gwen's rule was that children could pursue quiet activities like coloring, listening to music, or reading in the living room. She, as a busy pastor's wife, tried to maintain the living room as a place where unexpected guests could be entertained and where she could go to find quiet and order.

Even though the living room may be off-limits, it may still prove irresistible to even the most well-behaved little people. Keep fragile and irreplaceable things out of their reach. The mantel or a wall-hung case may be the best place to display your fragile pretties. You may have to wait a few years to display

them at all. Items made of metal or wood are fairly indestructible, but make sure your little ones won't cut themselves on sharp edges or have a heavy object fall on them.

Upholstery in the living room needs to be treated to repel stains. One man told Gwen he always kept paper towels under the sofa and chair cushions so that if something spilled, he could just whip out the towels and clean up the mess without running to the kitchen first.

Little ones like to pull on tablecloths, so consider that before using a floor-length table skirt and placing fragile objects on top of a table. Both Jo and Gwen can tell you from experience that before you know it, your children will grow up, and you will have many, many years to display fragile china figurines on tables with long skirts.

Now let's get to the nitty-gritty fun of creating a beautiful living room in your very own style.

Traditional

If you want a traditional style living room, one based on an earlier period than the twentieth century, there is a rich heritage of beautiful rooms to inspire you. Remember, however, that your room doesn't have to be purely from one era. If different eras are represented, the room will look like it has evolved over a number of years. If you have real antiques, use them. If you do not, there are many nice copies available—you can even build your own reproductions by ordering from two or three companies that provide ready-cut kits.[2] We often see traditionally styled furnishings at yard sales and in thrift stores. They usually need a little help to make them look great again, but that's all right because a shoestring decorator has more time than money. When she brings a beat-up old piece of furniture back to life she can say, "Look what I did."

Let's begin with a focal point: a bookcase full of hardback books; a tall piece of furniture such as an armoire, a china cabinet, or an antique secretary; or a fireplace with candlesticks on the mantel and a major piece of nicely framed art or a mirror hung above it. Often a focal point is simply a conversation grouping centered around an Oriental rug. Arranging the room and its art symmetrically around a focal point will give it a formal look.

The conversation group will consist of comfortable, upholstered sofas and chairs covered in elegant fabrics. Seating and pillows can be trimmed with fringe and piping. Pillows can be made with shiny or tapestry fabrics to add a more formal touch. You may not be able to upholster all the seating in exotic silks or damasks, but covering a few pillows with them will give the elegance without much expenditure.

You will need side tables near the upholstered seating. For one of her side tables, Jo uses a stack of art books. Gwen has an old, beat-up night table base with a round plywood board screwed to its top. She has used this as a side table in every house she's had by covering it with a round, floor-length decorator skirt. She often adds a topper of an antique, cutwork square cloth. (You can still find these wonderful cutwork and embroidered pieces reasonably, probably because they are too small for a table; but they are wonderful as table toppers.) If you don't have antique embroidery, you can layer one or two more cloths in shorter lengths of coordinating colors or prints for a custom look.

Traditional rooms look great with an Oriental rug or a well-made copy of one. They add pattern and a bright spot of color to the floor. Jo was fortunate to inherit one, so she planned her whole living room around it. Gwen found a beautiful red and dark blue one in a resale shop for a great price. Copies are reasonable in price. Hooked and braided rugs also add a traditional look to a room. Watch resale and thrift shops for those, as well. Area rugs are not necessary, but they do add a rich touch. You might try your hand at creating a reasonable copy by using fabric paints on a plain piece of carpeting that has had its edges bound or on a plain area rug.

Another traditional touch is gilt and silver frames. These can often be found at all the usual shoestring places. Most of them, however, need mending, patching, and regilding. You might find a great frame, but the picture may need to be replaced. A nice wooden frame can be painted, restained, or gilded using gilt paint found at craft stores.

It's not too difficult to construct an antique-looking screen to fill a corner or use as a room divider. Tri-fold screens are basically three large vertical frames hinged together. The panels can be painted and left open with fabric or lace gathered on rods within the open space. Screens can have thin masonite or particleboard attached to the frame that you can then paint, decoupage, stencil, or wallpaper. You can stretch canvas over the frame and use your artistic talents to decorate it. Gwen got an artistic friend to hand-paint her screen for her.

A traditional entry or living room can include something from the garden. It may be a garden seat that looks like marble, a painted iron garden chair, or a ceramic stool that you often see in conservatories. To add to a garden theme, you'll need lots of fresh or silk flowers lavishly displayed.

The traditional writing desk can be a table refinished in rich wood tones. Add a small lamp and accessories like a blotter and ink bottle to the top. Use a small table as a desk. It can also divide the room into separate areas.

Traditionally styled windows are treated with layers. The home seamstress is at a great advantage here. She can construct jabots, cornices, tailored valances, fringes, tassels, and heavy floor-length draperies quite easily. Drapery fabrics are ample and rich-looking and can be hung over lace or sheer curtains. A cornice or a tailored, gathered, or poufed valance will require less fabric than swags, which must be cut on the bias and therefore use a lot of fabric. If you don't want to sew, you can buy ready-made valances and glue on fringe, ribbon, or other trims.

Drapery panels that hang only beside the window and frame it without closing use much less fabric than those that close. Roman shades made in a very nice fabric that looks like silk, linen, or damask look very traditional. If the fabric is nice enough, it will look like a traditional valance when pulled up. Roman shades don't require as much yardage as drapes. Roman shades and miniblinds can be topped with a fringed valance, a cornice or a lambrequin to look more traditional.

Walls can be left plainly painted or enhanced with an interesting treatment. Richly toned colors sponged or rag rolled onto the walls looks great and adds a rich texture. Stenciled or wallpapered borders are appropriate. You could add real or stenciled moldings at the ceiling or chair rail, or picture frame style panels on the walls to add the final traditional touches.

Display any silver you have in a typical, traditional living room. You can pick up real silver, crystal, or glass accessories inexpensively. Shoestring sources are full of these kinds of objects. Gwen has purchased sterling silver pieces for almost nothing. Get a great silver polish and prepare to spend some time cleaning up your finds. Other traditional accessories may include large coffee table books, a tea or coffee serving set (in either silver or china) on a tray, antique or old books, and pretty collections of fine, old-looking things.

Tassels and fringes belong on pillows, drapes, lamps, and can be hung from doorknobs of cabinets and used on upholstery. You can find tassels on sale or make your own with embroidery floss. For cheap fringes, look in the usual shoestring places for old bedspreads or curtains with fringes on them. Even if the bedspread is worthless, the fringe may be in great shape. You can even dye the fringe to the color you need. If sewing on a fringe seems too hard, glue it on.

How to Make Tassels

1. Use one or more skeins of embroidery floss per tassel. The more skeins per tassel, the fuller the tassel will be. You may use just one color or a combination of colors to match your decor.
2. Remove the paper sleeve. Cut about a twenty-inch thread from one of the skeins, and set the piece aside. Cut off another piece about six inches long.
3. Gather the skeins into one bunch, ends even. Use the six-inch piece of floss to tie them all together tightly, exactly in the middle.
4. Fold the floss in half, holding on to the short middle string. Begin to wrap the remaining long piece of floss around the folded floss, close to the middle fold, holding tightly to the fold. (Leave a one-inch piece of the floss hanging out above the fold before you begin wrapping.) Wrap the floss around about ten times, and then tie it tightly to the one inch you left hanging out.
5. Use a small crochet hook or sweater snag remover to pull the ends down inside the tassel. Trim the ends of the tassel evenly.

Country

The country style can be very refined for a lovely living room. It is a nonpretentious look that is very welcoming. Upholstery is often in chintz or checks. To inexpensively create a country look, make slipcovers or add pillows and footstools covered in chintz, stripes, or checks. Wooden and wicker garden furniture with pretty cushions fit the country look.

Battenburg and other laces are often used generously in a country living room. Tables topped with floor-length cloths should have at least two layers, the top one being lace or white or another light color.

Combining patterns—checks, stripes, and prints—is popular in a country style. Use the suggested designer collections found in fabric stores, or design your own mix beginning with a floral print. Then choose a stripe, solid, and/or check in the strongest color in the print. Striped sheets come in handy here, not only for curtains but for creating slipcovers, chair pads, and pillows. Striped sheets are readily available in almost every color.

Country-style windows require lighter window treatments than windows in a traditional room. Try white wooden shutters, white sheers, lace, or pretty florals. A valance and side curtains in a cheery print or a solid can frame a window nicely. Miniblinds, a shade, or Roman shades can also be used for privacy and protection from the sun. You can pull them up under pretty toppers to hide them when not in use.

Walls in country rooms can be white, pastels, or the background color from the main print you are using—it can even be a strong color if you prefer. Gwen recently saw a strikingly beautiful country room with deep blue walls, white and wood-toned trim, and red patterned upholstery. Stencil painting, wallpaper borders, or wallpaper is appropriate in a country room. Installing real or faux trims at the ceiling and chair rail adds country details.

Make room for a display of country collectibles, and be sure to have some nice-looking books around. China pitchers used as vases and plants warm up the room. If you don't have a decorative pitcher, decoupage flowers onto a plain, inexpensive one. Add cheap baskets, which can be found in abundance in thrift stores. Buy the biggest ones you can find. Bigger looks better and can do double duty as storage.

Quilts are often used in country rooms to cover a chair, as a throw, or for display. Make your own quilt, or purchase one of those made in China and available everywhere. Watch thrift shops for worn quilts. They may be too expensive even in a thrift shop because quilts—old, new, or tattered—are highly prized right now. Combine scraps from your sewing with other fabrics in coordinating prints, and whip up a quilt for this room on the sewing machine. It won't need an inner layer of batting if it is only going to hang on the wall.

The kind of artwork used in a country room is important. The subject of your art could be plants (botanicals), farm scenes, rural themes, still lifes of fruits and vegetables, hunt scenes, portraits of animals, or someone's ancestors. Frame the art in heavy wooden frames without a lot of gilt. Your needlepoint and other needlework pieces look good on pillows here, but if you want to hang them on the walls, be careful to properly mat and frame them for the look of quality you are trying to achieve in your living room.

Use lots of pine and other wood throughout the room for chairs, tables, accessories, and folk art. Wooden floors would have a rag, braided, or floral print rug.

Contemporary

A contemporary look can be very sophisticated for your living room. Clean lines and minimal ornamentation give it a streamlined look. This living room could include a lot of glass and leather, built-in cabinets, Parsons tables, chrome, and natural elements like marble, wood, and granite on many surfaces. Be careful that not all lines in your contemporary room end up being square and straight. Include some graceful curves to add interest and soften the look. Curves could be in a table base, a chair's lines, a rug pattern, and art objects.

Include a variety of textures

Furniture in a contemporary living room is typically upholstered in solid colors. Use leather or natural fabrics with texture. The sculptured lines of furniture are highly valued in a contemporary look. Lack of clutter shows off all the elegant and graceful forms represented by the furniture and art in the room.

If you choose this look, work to make sure that it doesn't come off as cold, cheap, or unwelcoming. There are cheap-looking furnishings made in every style, but for some reason, the contemporary style seems to be a favorite of manufacturers of cheap-looking furnishings. Do your research at quality furniture stores.

Provide welcoming warmth with some soft seating and flowers in a simple vase with clean lines. Use large plants and trees, and bookcases full of books, art, and collectibles to add personality and warmth. A collection of spheres or other interesting objects can be displayed on a glass-topped coffee table. The table base could be a simple white box, a marble box, or a box painted to look like marble or granite using kits found in craft stores. You can also use glass bricks or one or two pedestals.

The focal point of the contemporary living room could be the same as in any style but with a contemporary interpretation. A fireplace with a striking piece of modern art hanging over it forms a focal point. So does a wall hanging, or gathering the conversation area around a boldly patterned rug or a big coffee table. You could arrange the furniture to take advantage of a fabulous view, and thereby eliminate the need for a piece of furniture to act as a focal point.

Window treatments in a contemporary room are minimal. Use mini- or vertical blinds, simple Roman shades, solid-colored tab curtains, or use no window treatment at all if you can get away with it.

Walls in a contemporary room need very little as well. Simple white or other neutrals work well. Grass cloth, linen, or other similarly textured walls add richness and keep the room from being too boring. Borders are rarely needed, and if they are used would be something clean and simple like a Greek key design.

Art for a contemporary room should be modern, unframed, or in simple frames. The art may provide the only color in a neutral-colored, contemporary room. Contemporary color schemes are usually neutrals: tans, gray, cream, beige, and the ever-popular black-and-white.

Floors can be bare tiles, marble, wood, or cement, and can be topped by area rugs where needed. If carpeting is used, it will usually be a low pile in even color. Berber carpets are popular in contemporary rooms.

Eclectic

The eclectic look is popular because you don't have to stick to one style. It is a mixture of styles and is what most of us end up with as we accumulate things we love from relatives, sales, and by shoestring shopping. It's a wonderful style because you can use whatever strikes your fancy. The trick is to retain unity of scale, color, pattern, and theme. It helps to achieve unity if all the woods are in the same or a very similar color. Repeating shapes, materials, and upholstery throughout the room brings it all together.

Jo's living room is eclectic. She began with the very traditional Egyptian rug, patterned with maroon and blue flowers and birds on a cream background. This rug has defined the colors and theme that unify her living room. She's painted the walls plain light cream. The windows have traditional cream valances over pleated shades that keep the draft out. Other traditional aspects of the room are a mauve wingback chair, silver candle holders with maroon candles in them, a display of bone china teacups and saucers, and the art hanging on her walls.

But Jo has also added many touches of country. Her side tables are wicker. There is a white ladder-back side chair with a blue cushion she borrowed from the dining room. The wholehouse garden theme is introduced in this room by cross-stitched, fringed, floral pillows. Her lamps and some bowls holding potpourri are white stoneware with blue flowers painted on them. She has several pieces of wooden folk art. Her father made a lovely wooden bowl and matching plate for her, and they are on display along with an old wooden cribbage set and an old wooden box that once belonged to her grandfather.

Her sofa and love seat are more contemporary in style but are the right scale to go with the wingback chair. With a camelback shape and mauve and blue in the fabric, they not only coordinate with all the red and blue in the room, but also provide comfy seating. The glass on the wicker coffee table lends a contemporary feel to the room. Large palms fill two empty corners.

Now that we've examined the living room, the next logical stop is the dining room. The formal dining room needs to be designed and decorated to have something in common with the living room, thus providing continuity.

Shoestring Tips

- Show off your nicest art.
- Display silver, nicely polished. Use it to hold potpourri.
- Glass items can give the look and shine of crystal.
- Rotate your displays occasionally.
- Display only hardback books in this room.
- Add brass coat hooks to a wide mirror frame in the entryway.
- Use an old milk can for an umbrella stand.

CHAPTER 11

Formal Dining Room

A Great Place to Honor Your Guests and Family

At this point you may be saying, "Hey! Wait a minute here! I don't have a formal dining room. I live on a shoestring. Remember?" Some shoestring decorators do have this room, and we don't want to leave them out. But even if you don't have a dining room, you will want to read this section, because there are ideas and tricks you can use in any room.

If you are fortunate enough to have a separate formal dining room, you can create a very lovely room with little expense. Like the formal living room, the formal dining room is a place to use your special pretty objects, fragile antiques, and fine-looking furniture.

If your formal dining room is part of the living room, treat the two areas as a continuous space. Use the same wall and window treatments in both rooms. A small table or judicious placing of the living room furniture will give an impression of separate rooms. Rugs can also help define the two areas.

Some of what you read in the rest of this chapter assumes you have a separate room for dining. Use what you can, and dismiss what does not apply to your situation.

The focal point of this room is usually the dining table and chairs. Often these can be found at all the usual shoestring places. Gwen has had two or three sets of chairs from thrift sources over the years. Her latest are the four Queen Anne chairs mentioned earlier. You will have lovely chairs when you refinish them using a rich wood stain. If you don't want to go to the trouble of refinishing your table and chairs, another alternative is to use any table and chairs you happen to have and cover them with fabric. By covering a table in a floor-length cloth and layering on another square cloth, you can create a luxurious table. Top it with glass and you won't have to wash the top cloth very often. You can also use coordinating place mats to protect the cloth.

You will find simple instructions for two kinds of floor-length tablecloths in library books and patterns. The easiest, and one that requires less fabric, is a simple circle cloth pieced together to reach the floor. The second type is skirted with gathered fabric. (See illustrations 11.1 and 11.2.)

Illustration 11.1
Floor length tablecloth style 1

Illustration 11.2
Floor length tablecloth style 2

Cheap Tip

To save money, sheets may be the least expensive way to get the amount of yardage needed for a floor-length tablecloth. Watch for sheets on sale. Muslin is also cheap and can be dyed or stenciled. Look in all the usual shoestring places for used bedspreads, sheets, or yardage. Jo once found six yards of wine-red satin at a thrift store and used it to make a Christmas tablecloth. Use fabrics with enough body to hang nicely. Sheer or flimsy fabrics don't work well.

Making a skirted, floor-length tablecloth:

To make this tablecloth, cut fabric the exact size of your table top plus one-half inch all around for seam allowance.

1. For the skirt, measure the circumference of the table and multiply it by 2.5. That's the length of the fabric you will need for the skirt. The width of the piece will be the distance from the edge of the table to the floor (usually about 30 inches) plus the width of the hem and a seam allowance of at least a half-inch. For example: Let us say we use a table circumference of 72 inches. 72 inches x 2.5=160 inches. If the distance to the floor is 30 inches, then we will add two inches to that and come up with the dimensions of fabric needed for the skirt: 160 inches by 32 inches.

2. Sew the short ends of the skirt fabric together to create a long continuous piece of fabric.

3. Hem one long edge, making a one-inch hem.

4. Gather the other long edge.

5. Adjust gathers evenly around the table top piece. Pin to the top piece and sew, using a half-inch seam.

By adding layers of fabric on top of one of these floor-length tablecloths, you can create a rich look. These added layers may include a table runner, a smaller tablecloth on top of the larger one, a doily under the centerpiece, and placemats.

Other Dining Room Furniture

If you have room in your dining room, a sideboard comes in handy. If you do not have a sideboard, use a dresser, a small table, a baker's rack, bookshelves that are about the right height, or a card table covered with a floor-length cloth. A brick and board creation covered with a floor-length cloth can look elegant. Even a shelf installed at the right height will do the job.

A china cabinet stores your pretty china and shows it off beautifully. If there is not enough room in the dining room, put the china cabinet in your living room or entryway as a focal point. Sideboards and china cabinets are truly showpieces and luxuries unless you buy them at a neighbor's garage sale or find a badly damaged sideboard and restore it. These pieces do not need to perfectly match your dining room set but should go with the overall style of the room. An old, painted breakfront or armoire would add character and do the same job.

Formal dining areas that are used only in the evening can be very dramatic. Drama is easy to create with deep-colored paint on your walls. Use a deep shade of your chosen color on walls and add a glaze with ragging or sponging to give depth and a little sheen. Move some large plants to the corners. Light some candles, close the drapes, and put on some soft music.

With just the price of a couple of cans of paint you have created a stunning room.

When dining formally, use large napkins of a good quality cloth. You can find white damask napkins at the usual shoe-string places and at antique stores. Lovely napkins can be made easily. Use a nice, natural fabric like linen or heavy cotton. Make them about twenty-four-inches square. Hem the edges. Hemmed edges will wear longer than zigzagged edges.

Large centerpieces in the middle of your dining room table look splendid in magazines, but in real life they prevent guests from seeing their fellow diners. Keep the centerpiece low enough to see over and around. You can still use a long or wide centerpiece, just not too tall. Or it is popular now to use several smaller table "centerpieces" down the length of the table, such as small bouquets of flowers in low containers, or several shorter, but fatter, candles.

Fresh, silk, or dried flowers are the usual mainstays for centerpieces. You might want to have several, seasonal imperishable centerpieces stored away for changes. Add candles to a centerpiece, and you have a traditional dining look. Other things can stand in for fresh flowers: a big bowl of fruit, a fall squash assortment, an appropriately-sized art object, a birdcage with vines and flowers intertwined through it, a potted plant in bloom, an advent wreath at Christmastime, a little vignette or arrangement of related things on a doily or bed of tulle.

A table runner down the middle of the table adds importance and interest to the whole effect. If entertaining, set your table the day before the event and decide what your centerpiece will be.

Low light—candles, turned-down lights, sconces, indirect lighting—adds to the drama. Shiny candleholders, shiny flatware, crystal, and other reflective surfaces give an elegant, formal touch and look spectacular. Add a dimmer switch to control how much light shines down on your dinner guests. If your chandelier is outdated or ugly, you can disguise it with paint. If it is beyond hope, remove it altogether until you can get one you like. Use candlelight instead, or put a floor lamp or two in the corners of the room.

Different Styles of Dining Rooms

Lets play with our three different styles of dining rooms to see how you can carry one style off. We won't list all the possibilities. Review our brief rundowns of different styles in chapter 2 for more ideas.

Traditional

Traditionally styled or antique furniture is usually the centerpiece of a traditional dining room. If you want a traditional dining room but don't have the right furniture, cover up what you do have. Use slipcovers on the chairs and a floor-length tablecloth on the table. No one will guess what's underneath. (See illustration 11.3.)

Add layers of fabric with runners and place mats. Choose brocades, linens, lace, damasks, and other rich traditional fabrics for these added layers. Trim them with cording and tassels. Set the table with silver or brass candlesticks or candelabrum, china, and a floral centerpiece.

Cover the walls with either floral wallpapers or borders. If opting for paint, choose a deep, rich tone. Try your hand at painting a mural on a wall. Stencil "moldings" at the ceiling and at chair-rail height. Layer dining room windows with heavy traditional treatments and finish with trims and tassels. On the floor, spread an Oriental-looking rug.

Illustration 11.3
Chair cover, traditional

A crystal or brass chandelier is the typical source of light. You may find one at the usual shoestrings places. Another alternative is to add tiny lampshades to your existing chandelier. More candles, flowers, and large silver or china serving dishes will top the sideboard.

Paint trompe l'oeil marble pillars on either side of the entrance to the dining room. Use masking tape and paint to create them, or nail up a one-by-twelve-inch board. Add wood trim at the top and bottom and give it a fake marble paint job.

Country

Natural finishes, wicker, and painted furniture are commonly used in a country dining room, but traditional furniture and antiques work here, too. Put ruffled floral cushions on the seats. As we mentioned before, any dining room set can have its style changed with the application of slipcovers and floor-length tablecloths. For a country look, use a cheerful floral fabric. Slipcovers for chairs will have gathered skirts detailed with ribbons and bows. (See illustration 11.4.)

Illustration 11.4
Chair cover, country

Old wooden tables and cupboards will fill in for the sideboard and china cabinet. A baker's rack or wicker étagére can fill the bill too. Display a collection of pewter or stoneware.

A large rag or braided rug on the floor will add the country touch. Often country floors are just bare wood. Use florals, lace, and ruffles on the windows.

Add country accessories in corners or on the sideboard. These might include baskets, wooden boxes, tins, brass candlesticks, or large pieces of folk art.

Lighting could be a brass, wrought iron, or a punched tin chandelier.

Paper the walls in country florals, or leave them white and stencil a country design on them.

Contemporary

A glass-topped table with a chrome or marble base is the usual contemporary dining table choice. But covering your table and chairs with tailored slipcovers in a neutral, nubby fabric will give the same impression of clean lines (See illustration 11.5.) Add wide grosgrain ribbon along the hems.

Recessed lighting, sconces, or a modern chandelier over the dining table work well in the contemporary room. Don't forget the candles. A block of wood given a stone finish works as a contemporary candleholder.

Walls can be painted and glazed to give them texture. Add one or two large pieces of modern art.

For a sideboard, a simple Parsons-style sofa table or another object about the same size covered with fabric will do the job. Or use two marble pillars topped with glass, or a board painted to look like marble, for an elegant sideboard. The china cabinet can be any cupboard you have. Give it an enamel-like finish in the neutral color of your choice.

Illustration 11.5
Chair cover, modern

Very few accessories are needed in a contemporary dining room. For those you do use, choose large, simple, and sculptured pieces.

If any window treatment is needed at all, make it simple with clean lines. Simple blinds below a tailored valance or cornice will fit the bill.

Dining Areas Disguised As Another Room

Sometimes a formal dining room that is used only once in a great while seems like a waste of valuable square footage. Your "dining room" may be put to better use as an office, library, den, music room, or sitting room. Dining in a room with book-lined walls sounds cozy and good to us. Somewhere in the room, employ a small table, drop-leaf table, or one of those units that look like a sideboard but extend with leaves to seat up to twelve people. After dinner, your extra room can easily be transformed from a dining room into whatever else you're using it for.

If you do not have a separate formal dining area for special occasions, you can create one in another room. Any room can be transformed. Use your entry or foyer for a dining room. Clean up your desk and hide the TV to transform your den into an eating area. Or put the dining table in the middle of your living or family room. Some other furniture may have to be temporarily hidden or taken to the basement for the occasion.

If this is the way you have to go, you'll have to find a dining table that works for this. Round tables about thirty inches in diameter can be used anywhere in a room—in a corner to hold a lamp or as a game table. When furniture is rearranged, put that table to use for dining. An oblong table can be used as a desk in an office or as a sofa table or lamp table at other times. A drop-leaf table unfolds and can be covered with lovely tablecloths to become a dining table. Tables that fold up into very little space can go almost anywhere. Even a card table can be pulled from storage and covered with a pretty tablecloth for a dinner party.

Use the chairs in the room and supplement with chairs pulled in from other rooms to create enough seating. Sitting in a wingback chair while dining sounds very elegant to us. Add candles and your nicest dishes and linens. Close the drapes and put on nice music and there you have it. Atmosphere is what counts, and a lot of that can be created with lighting and music—an inexpensive way to add a lovely touch to your home.

One of our friends had such a big dinner party that she needed to put two collapsible, round card tables in her master suite in order to seat everyone. The bedroom was on the same level as the kitchen so it worked, though it did feel a little strange sitting down to dinner in a friend's bedroom.

When Jo has a big dinner party and the guests can't all fit around her dinner table, she uses her adjacent living room as well. By removing the coffee table and putting the round outdoor table from her deck in the middle of the room, she can seat six more people. All the living room furniture gets pulled up close to the table, and she also pulls in other chairs from the bedrooms.

It is the atmosphere you as a hostess create with your attitude and servant's heart that will make a formal dining experience a success. Extra touches, such as place cards, tell your guests that you care. Make place cards by folding any heavyweight paper and adding art work, a stamped design, or a glued-on dried flower or bow. Tie a ribbon around the napkin and tuck in a flower. Shine your silver to add sparkle. The wonderful smells of the dinner cooking and background music will tell your guests they are important and welcome. Serve a cool drink and an appetizer in or near the kitchen to keep guests hanging around in the kitchen with you so you can talk with them easily. All these little touches welcome your guests and make them feel comfortable.

Shoestring Tips

- Light up a display of sparkling china, silver, or crystal.
- Put a dimmer on your chandelier to create a soft glow over the table.
- Install a narrow shelf to serve as a sideboard.
- For a formal table treatment, bunch up the corners of the tablecloth, tie with big bows, and add silk flowers.
- Make or buy washable covers or pads to protect upholstered seats.

CHAPTER 12

Kitchens and Eating Areas

Making the Most of the Place Where Family Gathers

Gwen's kitchen in Colorado Springs was a dream. It was spacious, cheerful, shiny, and new, and designed to her specifications. There was more than ample cupboard and counter space, plus a walk-in pantry. She even had a place to eat while watching the wildlife in her backyard. Jo was just a little bit jealous because she continues to live with a small galley-type kitchen with no windows, minimal storage, and even less counter space. Her counters are pretend-wood plastic laminates. The cabinetry reminds her every day that it's nearly twenty years old. Hopefully your kitchen more closely resembles Gwen's than Jo's. Whatever you have, though, it is full of potential.

Designers consider kitchens outdated after ten years or so. Remodeling them costs thousands of dollars. As shoestring decorators, we will not consider remodeling. We are going to work with what we have and make mostly cosmetic changes. Miracles can be done with paint, hard work, and a little Yankee ingenuity. There is even hope for Jo's kitchen.

Often a kitchen just needs brightening. After a while, the wallpaper or paint becomes dingy and worn and needs replacing. A quick coat of semigloss enamel on the walls and ceiling is probably the easiest way to brighten up a kitchen. We suggest gloss paint because walls in kitchens have to be washed now and then. Jo removed the orange and brown wallpaper that was in her kitchen when she moved in and applied a coat of semigloss white paint. Immediately her kitchen was brighter, looked bigger, and was more cheerful.

If you wallpaper, use washable vinyl. Stenciled or paper borders add style and interest to the kitchen. Just make sure that whatever you do ties in with any room that is open to the kitchen.

Gwen recently redid her parent's kitchen. Many years ago they had put a product known as Congoleum on the walls. Talk about durable! It is still there, and it is still bright. There was no question about peeling it off. Who knows what might be behind it? So what Gwen did was to put a coordinating paper—a pale green—in the adjoining eating area and then brightened it up by adding a border print of fruit on a dark green background. She put the border at ceiling height and at chair rail height in the eating area and then all around a wainscoting in the kitchen.

By using fancy paint finishes, you can make your dull kitchen walls appear to be lined with ceramic tiles, marble, granite, or stone blocks. With stenciling, you can create trellises of vines and flowers going up the walls and covering the ceiling. Paper borders are expensive, but with a little creativity and some time, you can stencil your own beautiful borders that are unique to your home.

Remember that kitchen wall art needs to be washable. Don't use oil paintings in areas that might get splashed. Prints should be framed and covered with glass. Don't limit yourself to "kitchen art." Monet looks great in a sunny kitchen! Adding classy, serious art gives your kitchen a richer look. Since most of us spend a fair amount of time in the kitchen, put wall art and objects you love there.

One of our friends recently painted her twenty-year-old kitchen, including the cabinets, a bright white and gave the whole room a new, cheery look. Painting the cupboards is a big job but worth all the effort it takes to do right. First remove the doors, drawers, and all the hardware—hinges, pulls, and handles. Be sure to keep track of where the doors came from so you will know where to reinstall them.

Except for parts attached to your walls, do the painting in the garage or outside. Wearing a mask and eye protection, sand first with medium sandpaper, and then with fine. Sand enough to remove all gloss. An electric hand sander is helpful here. Next, make sure all the surfaces are smooth. Fill any dents with

the appropriate kind of wood filler, and sand the filled spots so they are smooth like the rest of the surface.

Clean the surfaces thoroughly with a tacky cloth (you can buy these in paint stores). Then prime the wood with a coat of primer. Next apply a smooth coat of glossy paint. We like oil-based paint best, because it dries to a harder finish. After the first coat is dry, sand it lightly. (The instructions on the back of the can will tell you how long it takes for the paint to dry.) Clean with a tacky cloth again, then apply another even coat of paint. If you apply the paint too heavily, it will run and look awful and will take a long time to dry. It takes patience to apply two or three thin, even coats, but that's what works best. If you choose to use latex paint, sand lightly and apply one or two coats of clear polyurethane to protect the finish. We prefer gloss or semigloss for kitchen cabinets because it is more durable and easier to keep clean.

Paint all the surfaces of the doors, the front of the drawers, facing of the cabinetry itself, and the inside of cupboards. If you paint only the outside surface, the inside of the cabinets will still look bad. Paint applied to both sides of the wooden doors will prevent warping.

For a long time, we all had only white cabinets. Now, using paint you can duplicate almost any finish you can see or imagine. Deep colors are also a popular finish. To give a worn, antique look, sand paint lightly at the edges to show a little wood and cover with polyurethane.

If you like the look of wood, you can refinish the cabinets completely. Be sure to follow all instructions carefully on the can of stain. Jo's stained and varnished cabinets are showing age, so when the weather is warm she will remove all the doors, drawers, and hardware, sand all the cabinets with fine sandpaper, and apply two coats of polyurethane to revive them. This will be a lot cheaper than getting them refaced or replaced.

Sometimes all you need to update and change the look of your cabinets is new hardware. One of our friends wanted to paint her cabinets white because they looked so dark. Actually they were a nice, medium-toned oak. The hardware, however, was large, in a black Spanish style. She followed our advice and replaced all the hardware with smaller, shiny brass knobs and handles. The cabinets were miraculously lighter and brighter. Adding shiny new hardware may be just the pick-me-up your kitchen needs.

Kitchen Flooring

Flooring wears out in the kitchen because of the hard use it gets. A lot of traffic and things being dropped and spilled contribute to wear and tear. If your floor is wood, it can be sanded and refinished. Your options for redoing a wood floor include: staining, painting, or leaving the color of the wood natural and covering it with a durable finish.

After years of use, vinyl and linoleum floors literally wear out. At doorways and in front of the sink, the floors will eventually wear right through to whatever is underneath. Linoleum will pit and scar if something heavy is dropped on it, and it will scratch when a chair is dragged across it.

Carpeted kitchen floors get too dirty and stained for words. We do not consider carpeting a good choice for kitchens.

Ceramic and clay tile floors last a long time and wear well. They are easy to clean—although Gwen once had an all-white tile floor that showed everything, including water spots. The main drawback to tile is that it is so hard. This means it will be hard on your feet when you stand on it for long periods of time, and if you drop something breakable, it will definitely break. Tile and ceramic flooring are also noisier because they have no cushioning or sound-absorbing qualities.

If replacing your floor is part of your plan for redoing your kitchen, make your replacement choices carefully. Shop around for prices.

One way to save money is to lay soft linoleum or vinyl squares. If you do this, follow instructions carefully. The surface they go over must be perfectly smooth and clean. Every little imperfection and grain of sand will show after the floor has been walked on a bit. (Voice of experience here!) One of Jo's friends put new linoleum over old. The pattern in the old soon showed up in the new.

Laying linoleum and vinyl tiles is typically something a homeowner can do. Be sure to gather the correct tools, set aside more time then you think it will take, and get a friend to help. Prepare a cold meal ahead because you won't be able to cook or eat in the kitchen while working on it. Be sure to remove all the trim along the edges of the floor. You can either recycle the trim or replace it with new. If you plan to refinish the trim, do it while you have it off. Instead of removing the trim, a friend had her linoleum installed abutting the floor trim. It was cheaper and faster than removing it. Sadly, it looked awful. So do the job right!

When you have your flooring in place, you will want to protect heavy-use areas, like the space in front of the sink. Little semicircular rugs are sold for the purpose, but they wear out too soon and are too small. Bigger rugs look nicer and give you more protection. Jo uses a rug in a floral pattern that is about thirty-by-sixty inches to catch drips when the kids help out in the kitchen. The rug was only ten dollars at Wal-Mart. It gets vacuumed regularly so it stays clean. Gwen has a large rag rug that goes in the washing machine regularly. She has used the same rug for ten years. She uses a rubber sheet under it to keep it in place on the wood floor and to prevent slipping on it.

Kitchen Windows

A kitchen's window treatments should be washable. Fabric Roman shades or pleated shades are too hard to remove and clean. So keep them away from areas that get splattered. A lovely lace valance might be just the thing to tie your kitchen in with your country style rooms nearby.

If your kitchen needs sun control, metal miniblinds work well and can be adjusted to block the direct rays of the sun, yet still let in light. They can be wiped clean easily. Jo has wooden shutters in the opening between her living room and kitchen that is just above her sink. She spray-painted the dark shutters white. A regular dusting and wiping up of splashed food keeps them looking good.

If you have a windowsill wide enough to hold things, use it for an herb garden or other plants. You can increase the depth of your windowsill by adding a six-inch shelf the entire width of the window. Plants look better when you display an odd number of pots. All the pots should have some unifying theme or all be the same. Use the biggest ones that will fit on your sill.

Clay pots are cheap (you can find good ones in thrift shops). If you spray-paint them to match your decor, they will be nonporous and hold moisture better. Make sure your sill is protected with dishes under the pots. Porous clay saucers will not work because moisture will soak through them. Another idea for that sunny sill is a collection of colored bottles or other things that sunlight will enhance but not destroy.

Glass shelves can be installed across a window to give more space for plants or a collection. However, if you enjoy a lovely view or you want to watch the kids play while standing at the sink looking out the window, then you may not want to block your view.

Adequate lighting is vital in a kitchen. Install task lights above the stove and other work places or under cupboards.

Jo's previous kitchen had only one little ceiling light, eight inches in diameter for a big kitchen. It wasn't even in the middle of the room. She removed the tiny light fixture and had an electrician install a large fluorescent ceiling fixture in the middle of the ceiling. The hole left by removing the old fixture was patched, textured, and painted to match the rest of the ceiling.

Gwen likes lots of light—lots of windows, lots of lamps turned on day and night, and lots of task lights. She had matching punched-tin lamps installed over the stove in one house. In another, she put up the little fluorescent fixtures that either stick to the bottom of the cabinets or are attached with a couple of screws. She has installed dimmer switches for lights over tables so when company comes she can create a nice ambience, but when there is work to be done and she needs light, she can crank up the light to full power.

There are many pretty lighting options for kitchens. Lights can be recessed, halogen, fluorescent, or pendant. A visit to a lighting or hardware store will be enlightening (no pun intended!). Sometimes when people remodel, they sell their old light fixtures at garage sales or send them to Goodwill. Their castoffs may be just what you need. It's probably a good idea to hire an electrician to install or replace your light fixtures. If so, try to have several things for him to do when he comes because it will only take him a few minutes to hang your light, and you'll have to pay a basic fee for the first hour or half hour.

You might as well get several things taken care of all at once. If you opt to tackle the job yourself, remember to turn off the power before getting anywhere near the project.

Countertops

Countertops are a large part of the whole kitchen picture. If they are ugly, that is a lot of ugly to live with every day! There are several kinds of countertop surfaces. Laminates are an inexpensive alternative, and they come in every imaginable color. They even resemble all kinds of natural surfaces. Ceramic tiles also comes in a huge assortment of colors, styles, designs, and finishes. On the pricey side, there are the solid surface countertops that resemble natural products. Of course, you could use real marble, slate, or granite counters. We have seen countertops made of hardwood, also. The wood has to be properly treated so it will not absorb all the liquids that come in contact with a countertop. To install new countertops, you will have to remove the sink and reinstall it. So this is probably a job for professionals.

The do-it-yourself person can install ceramic tiles on an already existing counter top or backsplash. Gwen once installed some wonderful, decorative, and easy-to-clean tiles on the wall between the countertop and the cupboards above. The effect was delightful, and the project was not difficult. Most tiles come on netting to help in placement. Or you can purchase small, plastic tile spacers to assure perfect alignment of individual tiles not attached to netting. To install, apply glue to a prepared surface, lay down the tile and allow to dry, and then grout the spaces between the tiles and clean the whole thing up. Gwen likes to seal ceramic countertops with sealer to prevent stains from becoming permanent in the grout.

Laminated countertops pre-cut to size and ready to install are available at hardware stores or lumberyards. However, the choices may be somewhat limited. The hardware stores we visited keep only white, almond, and imitation butcher block in stock. Custom-ordered countertops will cost more, and having them installed will also be expensive. This may be one of those projects you have to save for. Or perhaps you know someone with whom you could barter to get the job done.

Organization Ideas

Too much clutter will sabotage any decorating scheme you may have. This is especially true in your kitchen. Lets look at ways to eliminate the clutter and make better use of your space.

We found it helpful to keep things organized according to specific tasks. Keep all the cooking things—pots and pans, cooking spices, utensils—near the stove. Keep all your baking things—flour, sugar, baking spices, salt, bowls, utensils, mixer, etc.—near the counter where you do all of your mixing and rolling out of dough. Keep everyday dishes near the dishwasher to make putting them away easier. Jo puts her everyday dishes into the cupboard below the counter, next to the dishwasher, to make it easier for the kids to empty the dishwasher and set the table without any help from Mom. Knives, colanders, cutting boards, and a trash container should be near the sink for easy cleanup after chopping. A canister, tin, or plant pot can sit prettily on the counter by the stove to hold long-handled utensils, and thus free up a drawer.

Gwen wanted a place to hang her copper pots in a tiny kitchen. There was nothing commercially available that would work in the small space she had, and most pot racks are expensive anyway. She found a length of copper pipe in her storeroom and cut it to fit between the cupboard and a beam in the kitchen. She attached it with brass fittings that looked something like what you slip a closet pole into. She cut the pipe with a hacksaw and made sure everything fit; then she cleaned the copper pipe with a high-quality copper cleaner, inserted it in the hangers, hung some purchased pot hooks over the rod and hung up her copper pots.

Declutter the area near your kitchen wall phone by hiding a small bulletin board with calendar, list of phone numbers, notes, or whatever you need on the inside of a nearby cupboard door, out of sight but handy for you.

A corner of the kitchen counter is often the dropping-off spot for mail and all the papers a family brings home. Those papers have to land somewhere, so you might as well accept it and plan for it. Set aside part of the counter to be a small office, or find room somewhere nearby for a tiny desk for papers, a phone, a bulletin board or message board, and perhaps a shelf for recipe books.

Think about ways you could add more counter space. Gwen once did it by replacing a worn-out wall oven and separate cooktop with a single drop-in oven unit. She freed up about four feet of counter space. An easier and less expensive solution would be to find a place to tuck in a small table, perhaps one with drop leaves that could be extended when you need them and folded down when you don't.

More storage is often found on the tops of cupboards. Often that space is used to show off a collection of things. But why not fill baskets, boxes, or tins with items you rarely use, such as your collection of holiday cookie cutters, gadgets, or even fancy table napkins reserved for special occasions?

We regularly go through our cupboards to see what we can thin out. With very little counter space, it is essential to keep

things off the top. A good rule is to donate anything that hasn't been used in the past year to a worthy charity. We like as many things put away as possible, not only because we need counter space, but also because things stored on the countertop tend to get splashed, dusty, grimy, and are in the way. For things that must stay out because they are in constant use, you may want to consider cloth covers to match your kitchen and keep your appliances clean.

Since visitors and family seem to gather in our kitchens, we need to make them as attractive as possible. Remember what we said earlier about tossing out anything that looks worn, tacky, dated, and cheap. It is better to have nothing decorating your walls than something tacky-looking. If you aren't sure your "treasures" pass the test, ask a very honest friend, whose taste you admire, to help you evaluate your kitchen accessories. Promise your friend that there will be no hard feelings no matter what she says. Keep your promise.

Often when we are shopping we discover something that we *just have to have* for our house. We are tempted to buy it, but that is when we have to ask ourselves these questions:

- Will it match what I have?
- Will it look dated and cheap in five years?
- Do I really need it?
- Can I easily afford to pay cash for it without blowing my budget?
- Can I make it instead of buying it?
- Can I buy it cheaper somewhere else?

If it passes all these tests, consider buying it. If it costs more than a few dollars, go home and sleep on it. If it doesn't pass these tests, then look at it for a few minutes, enjoy it, and then go on your way and forget about it.

There are a lot of little things that can be done quickly and easily to make your kitchen function better for you. Take the doors off one of the cupboards, fill in the holes where the hinges were screwed on, and restain or paint the cupboard. The open cupboard can be used to display a nice set of bowls, your everyday dishes neatly stacked, cookbooks, or one of your collections. To add a country touch, face the shelf edges with lace or put lacy cloths on the shelves and let the corners hang down. (See illustration 12.1.)

Consider installing spice racks in cupboard doors, adding lazy Susans for all the little things you need, or a large lazy Susan for that lost corner you can't see into or reach the back of. There is a myriad of other storage aids available at hardware stores: racks made of white-coated wire, stacking units for drawers, dividers for drawers, and full drawer organizers.

Install racks inside cupboard doors to hold lids, linens, spices, and small items. Use towel bars or self-stick hooks inside cupboard doors to hold dishcloths and towels. Jo put a clip on the inside of the cabinet door where her baking utensils are stored. The clip holds her recipe cards out of the way, yet at eye level, while she concocts goodies for her family.

A large hook screwed to the underside of a cabinet or a shelf in the pantry will hold your bananas so they won't bruise. A similar hook inside a lower door can hold a dishcloth or towel. Hanging cups and mugs on cup hooks frees more shelf

space. Lining shelves with contact paper or rubberized shelving material makes them easy to clean and gives them a clean new look. If you find a roll of vinyl-coated wallpaper in a thrift shop or a close-out bin at the wallpaper store, use that for shelf paper. It's more durable than shelf paper and cheaper.

Eating Areas

An informal eating area is often an extension of the kitchen, not only in form, but in function as well. This is typically where the family dines, does art projects, and works on homework. Some food preparation may also be done at the table. Jo has a tradition in her home of decorating Christmas cookies. Actually the kids do the decorating. They use the table in the informal eating area and make a lovely mess of things. When she makes scones or cookies with the help of a little person, she brings the mixing bowl and ingredients to that table so the little person can help out.

An eating area that adjoins or is part of the kitchen will be decorated like the kitchen. Use the same paint, carry through with the same wallpaper border or stencil, and have the window treatments either the same or coordinating. The flooring should be the same, too. This room often gets the same rough wear and tear as the kitchen, so it needs the same durable surfaces.

The main furniture pieces in a kitchen eating area are the table and chairs. Because they are constantly used, they need to be sturdy. Since this is not a formal space, mismatched things can add interest and fit just fine. Even though all the chairs may be different, by painting them the same color or putting matching chair pads on all the chairs, you can create a unified look. A pretty tablecloth and flowers for the middle of

Illustration 12.1
Group illustration of 2 shelves decorated

the table keep it looking pretty even when not in use. If this area has adequate natural light, add some greenery for a nice atmosphere; use silk plants for rooms without much light.

Kitchens and eating areas need a light touch without too much fussiness because of their heavy traffic. To display a collection in this room, it might be wise to use a wall that has plenty of room for people to pass by without brushing things off a shelf. Think about adding a shelf one foot from the ceiling and extending it the whole length of a wall. You can even run it all around the room. This is a great place to safely display an attractive collection. You can even display china pieces here because they will be well out of the way.

Is there room for a hutch, plant stand, shelves, or other decorative furniture? Don't squeeze too much in, but if there is room for added storage pieces, go for it. Perhaps this is where you will find the needed corner for a small desk. Remember, you need about three feet behind each chair so you can scoot out and sit in easily.

Lighting is important in this room because a family uses the table often. A chandelier can offer light, but before you buy one, check out how much light it will give. Gwen has a punched-tin light fixture with eight arms to hold candles. The fixture also has a downlight, and she found that a small flood-light in the fixture does a great job of providing enough light not only for eating, but also for working on projects or for paying bills. Hang the light fixture thirty-six inches above the table-top or even higher if the people living in your home are all tall to avoid bumped heads.

It doesn't take much to give this eating/study area definite style. Regardless of what you have, by adding the right details you can make your kitchen and informal eating area any style you like. Let's see how.

Traditional

Achieving the look of a traditional kitchen requires the same touches you would include for any traditional room. Use a fabric window treatment for any window that needs dressing up. Just remember the inevitable splashes and spills, and interpret your traditional-looking window dressings in washable fabrics. Tassels and fringes are not needed here, but cording, ribbon, or other less fussy trims are still appropriate. A full, gathered valance or other topping about fourteen to nineteen inches long over blinds will do the trick.

Cabinets can be painted and antiqued to look as if they have been around a long time (and maybe they have!). Frame doors in wood trim. Add chair rails and crown moldings. Replace door and drawer pulls with brass or antique replicas.

Paper walls with a traditional floral wallpaper or border. The same effect can be created by stenciling. For really old-looking walls, stencil the walls to look like large blocks of stone. For wall art, use prints in gilt or antique frames.

To furnish the eating area, use antiques or replicas. Since this is not a formal room, mismatching is OK. A wrought-iron table and chairs made for outside use will give the air of a traditional conservatory. All you need to add are plenty of plants and flowers.

To achieve a traditional look, light fixtures may merely require a change of a globe or the addition of tiny shades. There is a wide selection of globes and small shades at hardware and lighting stores.

Floors in a traditional kitchen are of natural products like slate, marble, wood, or clay tiles. A classic look that works for any style, but especially for traditional, is the black-and-white checkerboard tiles. Whether you have a truly traditional floor or vinyl flooring, use a large fake Oriental rug on the floor to add that final touch.

Country

There are two philosophies to country kitchen decorating:

1. See how many antiques and collections you can display on every available surface.
2. Use country details with restraint to decorate—almost a Spartan look.

The first philosophy is for people who don't mind living with clutter and the need to clean all that stuff on display. It's for those who don't mind working around the things on countertops and tables. The second is for those of you who do not like cleaning lots of things, who need a tranquil environment, and do not like having to move things to work at the kitchen counter. Some of you may be somewhere between the two extremes. Let's talk, in general, about how to add country charm to your kitchen and eating area, and you can decide how many antique kitchen gadgets, baskets, copperware, and brown jugs you want on display.

Simple wooden furniture that looks as if it lived in a farmhouse kitchen says country. Popular now are solid oak sets. Having a mismatched set adds country personality, so watch for good, sturdy pieces at favorite shoestring shopper places. A lace doily under a Mason jar of wild flowers finishes off the table. A pie safe, hutch, or other simple wooden piece can add extra storage in a country kitchen. White painted furniture with nicks and scarred edges, or a cracked finish, are currently popular. Old is new again.

A valance of lace, checks, plaid tea towels or even an old, flowered forties' tablecloth can give a country look to your windows. Also popular are simple or ruffled curtains in solids, gingham checks, or a country floral. A wonderful finishing touch is one or more pots of flowers and plants on the windowsill. Geraniums—real or silk—add a delightful touch to any country kitchen.

Themes in a country kitchen may include farm animals, checkerboard patterns, flowers, fruits, and vegetables. You can choose any country theme you like and stencil it everywhere. Wallpaper books abound in patterns for the country decorator. Look at them for inspiration; it is fun to mix prints and patterns in a country kitchen and dining area.

To give your cabinets a country look, replace the pulls with white ceramic ones. Give the woodwork an antique finish. Take a door or two off a cupboard and display country cookware that you really use. Country cabinet doors often have insets of chicken wire, punched tin, or glass.

If you plan on replacing the floor, brick and wood are the usual country choices. Add a braided or rag rug to whatever floor you have.

As you can see, country can be simple with only Battenburg lace at the window, a simple flower arrangement on the table, and a rag rug on the floor. Or it can be made fussy with prints and collectibles everywhere. With country, there is a lot of room for personal expression.

Contemporary

If you like clutter, do not use contemporary as your style. The contemporary kitchen is clean-lined, modern, shiny, and uncluttered. Only a few shiny modern appliances will be found on countertops.

Cabinets require a simple, shiny finish. Highlight the natural beauty of wood with a natural finish. Or use a high-gloss enamel to paint on a neutral color. Use simple pulls on the drawers and doors if you use any at all. Windows need only minimal blinds. Display flowers or plants on the windowsill in simple containers, but only display one or three plants, with plenty of space between them. Art on plain walls need to be neatly framed. This will add color to an otherwise neutral scheme.

A black-and-white checkerboard tile floor, wood, clay or ceramic tile, marble, or linoleum imitating these adds contemporary style. And do not forget to add a large rug with a bold pattern.

Choose simply styled chairs and a table in wood, metal, or glass. If pads are needed for the chairs, use fabrics in a solid or geometric print. The total look should be uncomplicated, clean, and sophisticated.

Shoestring Tips

- Clean out and declutter cupboards and countertops.
- Get organized.
- Remove all the kitchen art from the walls. Replace with nicely framed and matted prints that match your kitchen decor.
- Clean out the bugs and dirt from your light fixtures.
- Put a plant or flowers on the kitchen table, and under the flowers place a doily, table napkin, or scarf that matches your kitchen style.
- Replace the kitchen rug with a larger one for more color and better protection.
- For a new valance, drape dish towels, table napkins, or a tablecloth over a curtain rod. Overlap napkins over the rod for a unique look.
- Install a shelf over the window to display a collection.
- Find some decorative boxes, baskets, or large glass jars to store little-used things.
- Use mirror hangers to install a piece of clear acrylic behind the range to protect wallpaper.

CHAPTER 13

Den or Family Room

Where We Really Live

The family room or den is a place for relaxation. It's the family's hideaway from a busy world. Therefore, it will probably not have the formal mood of the living room. In most homes, this is the room where the family really lives.

What goes on in your family room? For the Janssens, this room functions as a place to watch TV and videos, listen to music, play the piano, play games, read, visit with one another, and pay bills. This is where they spend most of their waking moments together.

All these activities require comfy furniture, lots of good lighting, bookshelves, a desk, a piano, a large-surface coffee table, a TV and VCR, and cabinets for the storage of games, music, and craft supplies.

How do you want this room to function in your house? Are some activities being done in your family room that you want moved to another room? Are there some activities taking place in other rooms that you want moved to the family room? It's a good idea to sit down with your family and decide how you want your family room used. As children grow up, the usage of this room will change. When children are small, it's a playroom. When they are school-age, it's a place for homework. When Jo was homeschooling her kids, her family room served as a classroom. When kids become teens, the family room is often used for parties with friends.

What do individual members need in this room? Some family members want to quietly read and watch TV. That means you'll need an ottoman or two, a place to set snacks and reading material, and adjustable lighting. If you plan to play board games, you will need a table to play them on and nearby storage for the games.

If you plan to watch TV, place the chairs and sofas at comfortable distances and angles for viewing the screen. If you will occasionally be entertaining friends in your family room, make the seating arrangement work as well for conversation as it does for viewing TV. It needs to be comfortable.

Are some of your family members more comfortable on the floor? Get some big floor pillows and slip them into removable, washable covers. Gwen made a floor pillow by filling a big square of pillow ticking with the stuffing from old pillows that had been washed and dried. Then she covered the floor pillow with fake fur. Twenty years later that floor pillow still looks like new.

Include plenty of pillows and an afghan or throw to cut the chill on a dark and stormy night. Make sure nappers can have a full pillow without having to go to a bedroom to get one. For the sofa, Gwen likes full-sized pillows in zippered pillowcases of a dark-colored fabric that doesn't show soil.

If the kitchen table is between this room and the kitchen, it will often function as part of the family room. That is probably where homework and craft projects will be done, so plan for adequate lighting and storage of supplies nearby.

Above all, everything in the family room needs to be very durable. Choose upholstery fabrics that will hide stains well and that have a finish that repels soil. One of our friends uses leather for her family room seating because it wears so well and nothing will stain it. Leather is expensive but will last almost forever. Consider it a long-term investment, and save for it. Tables and other wooden furnishings also need to be sturdy and have tough finishes. Jo's coffee table is solid, unstained oak coated with several layers of a clear, waterproof finish.

Sturdy furniture is best for a family because it is safer. It will not collapse when junior learns how to climb on top of it and Uncle Bob sits on it. *Everything* needs to be able to withstand considerable weight. Remember Jo's first sofa—the cheap one? A couple of the Janssen's friends are former NFL linemen. That poor little sofa visibly and drastically sank when they sat on it.

Take a look at your family room from the standpoint of safety. Are there other safety hazards? How about the bookshelves? Jo uses brackets to bolt her tall bookshelves to the wall and ceiling to prevent any visiting toddlers from turning them over on top of themselves when they try to climb them. Make sure there are no cords to trip over or unsteady lamps to come crashing down. All window treatment cords must be kept wrapped on cleats or in some other way kept out of toddlers' reach.

You may need a lot of storage for the all the electronic equipment, books, movies, games, art supplies, and music that need to be stored in your family room. One big unit that does it all is ideal, but putting together a couple of smaller matching units (or refinishing a couple so they will match) will serve the purpose just as well. Surrounding a fireplace with shelves and cabinets will emphasize the fireplace as a focal point.

For a wall unit look, you can purchase several individual pieces and combine them. Put the TV in the middle and surround the TV unit with less deep units to create a whole wall of storage. The TV will extend out further than the rest of the units. These separate pieces can be bought and rearranged in endless ways to meet your needs. Bookshelves can go on top of deeper units that have doors that conceal storage space. For this purpose, you can recycle kitchen cabinets with countertops still attached. Top with a shelf unit. Remember, we use things because they function well for our needs, not necessarily for their originally intended use. *Think creatively.*

Sometimes a den or family room must also serve other functions. It may also be the guest room or an office. Using a sofa bed or daybed makes this room more versatile. A desk in a corner or along a wall will help with office needs. But if at all possible, keep your family room for your family's time together.

Your overnight guests will be more comfortable elsewhere in your home, and whoever needs the office will get more done if the desk is in another room.

If you have a large family room, resist the urge to line the walls with seating. Remember it's all right to float furniture in the center of the room. Create conversation areas and reading corners. Place seating in front of the fire or TV. Be mindful of traffic patterns—make sure people can walk around comfortably without blocking the TV. Use the walls for storage, a game table, a desk, a piano, an entertainment center, or a sound system and not as a place against which to push furniture.

This room is a good place to display your less fragile collections. The mantel, a corner, the bookshelves, the hearth, and a sofa table all offer places to display things like a collection of old teddy bears, colorful water pitchers, folk art, travel mementos, antique toys, and touchable antiques of all kinds (radios, cameras, doorknobs, etc.) These make good conversation starters, tell something about you, and give personality to your room.

Wall art could include maps, a quilt, a collage you have made of travel brochures collected on your trips, or a nicely framed print. This room is also a good place to show off your photography or your children's artwork. If they are well-framed and matted, they will look much better and very important. One of Jo's friends changes the art in her wide, rich-looking frames whenever her daughter brings home another fitting masterpiece from art class.

If you do not have any tall furniture in your family room you may need to add height. To do this, fill a couple of corners with plants, a tall narrow storage unit, a corner cupboard, a grandfather clock, or a screen. It's a great place for an armoire or an old-fashioned cupboard. For country decorating these pieces can be quite primitive.

How do we tie all these elements together? In the usual way: with color, themes, and motifs. Jo's family room uses a blue-and-white color theme to pull everything together. As with many of her rooms, books and flowers prevail.

Here are a few other touches to add to your family room:

- A ceiling fan will keep a family room cool in summer and force down warm air in winter. Add a light to the fan to improve overall lighting.
- Hide all electronics behind the doors of an old wardrobe or TV cabinet.
- Use a glass top on fine wood side tables for protection. Any glass shop can cut these to size and bevel the edges to make them smooth.
- A sheet of glass on a base of just about anything is a cheap coffee table. The glass is impervious to stains and will also take up less visual space.
- Stencil or paint a favorite quotation or Scripture verse near the ceiling.
- Install track lighting to remove the need for so many lamps and side tables.
- A floor cloth or inexpensive area rug will give warmth to your toes and help define areas.
- A fake fireplace can be made for a focal point for an otherwise dull room. Create a mantel and surround. Put a plant or fire screen where the fire would go, top the mantel with a collection and a big picture. (You can now buy gas fireplaces that need no chimney or venting. They are safe but expensive. It would, however, be cheaper than having a fireplace installed. It might be worth considering if your family loves to have a fire.)
- Use garden furniture for side tables and extra seating.

- Particleboard decorator tables, preferably the thirty-inch size, are a good choice because they're inexpensive and there's not much you can do to hurt them. The floor-length and layered tablecloths can be washed and changed to suit the mood or season. A glass top cuts down on washing the cloths.
- Footstools and ottomans are not only for feet. You can set a tray of goodies on an ottoman. Low ottomans and footstools can be slipped under the coffee table and pulled out for extra seating when you have a full house.
- Put cushions on a raised hearth for more seating.
- Look for thrift-store finds to serve as a coffee table. Remove the handle from a wagon and top the wagon with glass for a table. A plain pine box or a trunk makes a good coffee table.

Now you have the challenge of decorating your family room in a way that works and does what you need it to do with style. Even though we use family-resistant furnishings, they can all come together to look decorator beautiful.

Traditional

In a traditional family room, we will not use the same fine fabrics we would in a traditional living room, but we will include many of the same details. Classic and curvy furniture is appropriate here as in the rest of the house. But here we will upholster furniture in more durable and low-care fabrics. Throw pillows and cushions will still be outlined with fringes and cording. The colors will remain rich. Side tables will need a coating of polyurethane or another tough finish to make them impervious to sweaty glasses of lemonade.

Television sets don't look very traditional, so hide yours behind the doors of an old wardrobe or TV cabinet. The piece will probably be large enough to serve as a focal point for the room. Gwen hides her TV, VCR, and sound system in a large, traditionally styled bonnet-top cabinet and finds it is absolutely wonderful to be able to close the doors on the cabinet and hide everything away.

In a traditional family room, collections on display might include items made of brass, pewter, or wood. Antique cameras, radios, binoculars, ink bottles, dolls, stuffed animals, Noah's Ark sets, inlaid boxes, snuff or pill boxes, sailboats, travel mementos, or clocks fit in well.

Adorn cushions, tablecloths, and window treatments with fringes, trims, and tassels. Layers of fabric at the windows and on tables and cushions help define the family room as traditional.

Use the walls to give the room a more traditional feeling. Stencil them to look like they have framed wall panels. Stencil chair rails and ceiling trims. Add a wall or two of old-looking books to give the room the feel of a traditional library.

The usual Oriental or Persian rug would look great in this room, but you may want to use an inexpensive imitation instead of the real thing.

To add height, make a screen for a lonely corner. Decoupage postcards or copies of old family photos to the panels.

Country

The country family room or den will be a cheerful, comfortable place full of flowers and folk art. The furniture will include sturdy wooden pieces, garden furniture, and wicker. Upholstery will be pretty, but durable.

The focal point may be whatever houses your TV or a fireplace. If the fireplace is your focal point, put a rug in front of it, country collectibles on either side of it, and a collection of some kind on the mantel. Over the mantel, hang a large picture, three antique rifles, an oak-framed mirror, or some large, interesting country collectible. Add an antique lantern or candles in wooden candleholders on both ends of the mantel. Gwen's country family room mantel holds a set of wooden blocks that spell, "Welcome Friends." Her candleholders were originally factory spindles for yarn.

Have fun showing off your collection of toys, farm tools, rag dolls, or other country household items. Display them as parts of a vignette, fill corners with them, or decorate tabletops and shelves with them. Gwen has her daughter's Raggedy Ann and Raggedy Andy on display, along with a homemade checkers set she picked up in a thrift shop in a mining town in Colorado. The board is the end of a dynamite crate.

Use a lot of durable, cotton country prints on windows, tables, pillows, and seating, following our simple formulas for mixing prints found in chapter 6. Mattress ticking is a sturdy striped fabric. Denims and other thick cottons will provide you with long-wearing solid colors. Denim is a trendy family-room upholstery material right now. Be generous with lace, ruffles, ribbons, and bows. These fabrics and trims wash well, are inexpensive, and usually prove durable.

Make a tall folding screen of fence pickets. Nail together three panels with several pickets on each panel. Attach hinges or drill holes at the top, bottom, and middle to wire the sections together. Paint the screen white and decorate with silk flowers and vines or stenciled bird houses. (See illustration 13.1.)

Contemporary

Even with the clean lines and lack of clutter of contemporary design, you can still have all the cozy comfort you need.

Your furniture for a contemporary family room will be simply designed, but sturdy and comfortable.

Use fabrics with interesting textures to keep the room from being boring. Choose nubby natural wool, corduroy, denim, and woven man-made fabrics. Add piping to give it more detail and style.

Jo's brother has a contemporary-style family room. His comfortable, overstuffed sectional sofa is upholstered in blue. There is a huge matching hassock for extra seating or for feet. The sofa faces a wall of white, built-in storage units designed to hold books, collectibles, and the TV. Cupboards below are for storage. Simple vertical blinds cover the windows. The plain white walls are adorned with a couple of large, simply framed pieces of art. The floor is covered in off-white Berber carpeting. It is a simple recipe for contemporary comfort.

Track lighting looks very modern and will lessen the clutter on side tables in your contemporary room. Those side tables can be simple Parsons tables, wooden cubes, or pillars of fake marble topped with glass. Even in a contemporary family room, you need somewhere to put your movie snacks.

Accessories of good quality with clean lines will add more warmth and interest. Use paint and special techniques, such as spray-on stone or marbling, to make ho-hum things look great. Books belong in a family room regardless of style. Bookcases painted white will look clean and cool.

The family room is a great place for all your family members to gather for time together. But in the midst of the noise and confusion, you often need a quiet retreat. That place can be your master bedroom. Read on to learn how to make your own special haven.

Illustration 13.1
Picket fence screen

CHAPTER 14

Master Bedroom

A Special Refuge

When Gwen is buying a house, one of the first things she looks at is the master bedroom. That room is her haven, her special refuge, the place she goes to rest at the end of the day. Recently Jo and Al looked at a house that had four small bedrooms upstairs. Jo's first thought was, *If this were my house, I'd knock out a wall between the master bedroom and a spare bedroom and make this one gigantic room with windows all around.* That is exactly what Gwen has done in her latest house.

The master bedroom is often a showplace of opulent comfort. Today's new homebuilders are including balconies, vaulted ceilings, reading corners, entertainment centers, fireplaces, and large bathrooms in the master suites. It makes a nice little getaway. Although you may not have any of those luxuries, you can still create a comfortable, relaxing, and even romantic refuge—a retreat for yourself and the one you love (if you're blessed enough to have one).

Because this room doesn't get a lot of rough use, it's another good place to use and display antiques or valuable, fragile things. The beautiful rug that you don't want any stains on, the fragile figurines, and cut crystal vase you received as a gift can safely be used in the master bedroom. In fact, these fine things may be the clues and direction for the color scheme in this room.

The focal point of the master bedroom is usually the bed. Popular now in these luxurious suites are four poster beds. They look grand and romantic. Unfortunately most rooms cannot accommodate a bed this large, and we don't advise buying a new bed just because it is fashionable. You can create the look of a canopy and the height of a four poster with valances and curtains hung from the ceiling. Sheets provide shoestring-priced yardage. A curtain rod will fit right through the double-folded hem. You will need a lot of fullness for a rich look. Try doing what Jo did—put a valance and curtain at the head of the bed. The valance and side curtains extend only a foot from the wall. (See illustration 14.1.) It looks romantic and doesn't use very much fabric. She used white sheets for the curtains and

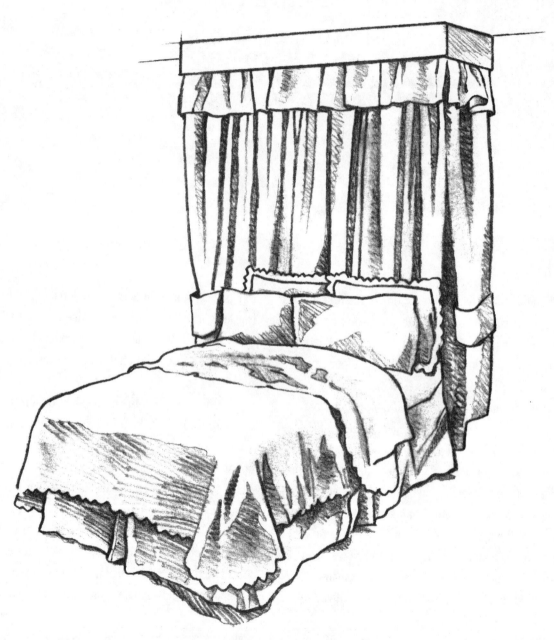

Illustration 14.1
Bed with valance and false canopy

found the Battenburg lace valances on sale. If you do curtain your bed in grand, old-royal style, use the same kind of curtains on your windows to tie it all together. All that fabric will accumulate a lot of dust over the years, so you will have to vacuum, clean, or wash it all from time to time. If you are allergic to dust you may want to avoid this idea!

Headboards can be pricey, but we see a lot of them at all our usual shoestring places. They are just waiting for someone to creatively transform them into the perfect headboard. Paint, stencil, decoupage, or stain one to suit you. You can make or reupholster a fabric headboard with the help of a staple gun or tacks. Someone gave Jo a king-size bedspread once. She only had a single bed. So she cut enough off to make a bedspread that just fit her bed and had plenty left over to recover her old, worn upholstered headboard as well.

You don't even have to start with a "real" headboard. They can be rigged from many things. You can make your own bent-willow headboard (very trendy right now) by bending thin branches in an arch and attaching them with long staples to a backboard at the bottom. Or paint a headboard on the wall for a whimsical look. Hang a quilt, wall hanging, or rug behind the bed. Attach big pillows to a rod on the wall. Pile up a bunch of pillows against the wall. Use picket fencing or cut a shape you like from plywood and paint it or pad and upholster it.

Often we see beds that are a little lower than the new beds at furniture stores. New ones are about twenty-five to thirty inches high. A low bed doesn't make much of a focal point in the master bedroom. Raising the bed a few inches or even as much as a foot will make it look better, richer, and more important in the room. There are elevating devices on the market to give a bed a lift, or you can build a strong platform and put the bed on it. If you use a long bed skirt on the bed it will cover the platform, and you won't even have to carpet or paint it. Whatever you do, don't put the casters on a stack of books. The bed will roll off and could cause injury. To add height and comfort to your mattress, add a layer of foam or an egg-carton cushion. A fluffy comforter adds height too. A large picture or wall hanging—a half canopy, for example—on the wall at the head of the bed adds visual height and importance to the whole bed.

Bedside tables are needed for all those little things we like to have next to us at night. You need to know that it is difficult to find bedside tables tall enough to be useful if you have a high bed. Gwen's bed is about thirty-five inches high, and every bedside table she owned looked funny beside it. She solved the problem by purchasing two round decorator tables with long legs, covering them with a fabric that matched the tab curtains in the room and topping the tables with glass.

For a master suite, you want attractive tables. Round decorator tables with double layers of cloths look soft and pretty. If there is room, use the thirty-inch diameter rather than twenty-inch kind because it will look so much nicer and give you plenty of room for books, magazines, a lamp, and all the other accoutrements to make your private hideaway special. We found some thirty-inch diameter ones at a linens store that have a built-in shelf underneath. Even without the shelf, the area beneath the skirts can be used for storage or to hide stereo speakers. There are also half-round tables on the market that do not take as much space as round ones. They fit closely against the wall. You can also use a small desk beside the bed, or even a chest of drawers.

If you are putting tables on both sides of the bed, they do not have to match perfectly (that can be pretty boring), but keep them at about the same height, bulk, or visual mass. Adding things to the top of the tables and pictures above them also affects their overall visual weight. Balance in a room is restful to the eyes, and your bedroom should be the most restful place in the house. If you are unable to put a table beside the bed and really need space to put a clock and a tissue box, simply attach a small shelf to the wall next to your bed at the right height.

If you like to read in bed, then you need adequate bedside lighting. Matching lamps on either side are a typical solution. Lamps that are about the same size and shape with matching shades will work. Lamps and their shades can be painted or decoupaged to match each other and tie in with your decorating scheme. Wall-mounted swing-arm lights or hanging lights will free up table space. Hanging lights don't have to be much more than pretty shades. Get a hanging light kit at any lighting store and assemble the hanging lights yourself. The kit comes with electrical parts, a hanging chain, a switch, and a couple of ceiling hooks. Add a pretty shade for a decorative look.

The master bedroom might be the ideal place for a reading corner. Imagine enjoying a quiet time in your retreat away from the rest of the family. Begin with a comfortable reading chair. A chaise lounge would be elegant, but a comfy chair and a footstool that can be tucked out of the way when you are not using it is just as good. A lamp and some place to put your coffee and reading glasses complete the reading corner. Even if you don't intend to read in the master bedroom, you may want a chair where you can sit while you put on your shoes. Jo often uses the chair in her room as a place to drape clothes when she doesn't feel like hanging them up late at night!

Other seating alternatives are: a bench, an old trunk, a small sofa, or other similar piece placed at the foot of the bed.

Jo keeps her Mom's old cedar chest at the foot of her bed. The top holds her decorative bed pillows and her robe when she is sleeping. Inside are extra blankets. A chest or trunk does double duty as seating and storage. Foot-of-the-bed seating can be wide enough to span the entire foot of your bed or be as short as a vanity bench. Since it is at the foot of the bed, it will not take up much space.

Closet space and storage are often a problem in a bedroom. You can store things in boxes under the bed or on high shelves, of course. But those aren't the only places to store things. Decorative bandboxes, covered boxes, and baskets with lids can store things in plain view. These containers will add detail and personality to a corner or when put under a dresser or side table. Make a regular habit of cleaning out your closets to keep up with the never-ending addition of clothes and accessories.

Windows and walls in the master suite will depend on your ambience and style, of course. Fancy paint techniques—ragging and sponging—and wallpapers add to the look of luxury. Windows need to be dressed for privacy and light control.

A dressing table is a nice feminine touch. Any small table can be covered with a skirt and a mirror added above it. Put pretty bottles, nicely framed photos of loved ones, silver, glass, or crystal things on top, and a small lamp on one side.

It's not hard to build a dressing table. Just attach a board to the top of two filing cabinets or anything that is the right height. Make a skirt for the front of it and attach with hook-and-loop tape. Congratulations, you've just created another place to store things: under the skirt. To dress up a chair for your vanity, put a matching skirted pad on the seat. If you don't have a chair, borrow one from the dining room. You can whip off the skirt and return it to the dining room for those rare formal dining times. If a skirted table is not your style, put a small table or desk to work. After refinishing it, top it with flowers, a little lamp, or pretty boudoir accessories. Attach a mirror to the wall over it, and you have transformed a desk or table into a vanity.

Bedspreads and comforters are expensive. They can, however, be found at all the usual shoestring places. King-size spreads can be cut down to fit a smaller bed. If the spread is too small, add a ruffle or trim to make it bigger. You'll want to wash a used spread before putting it on your bed, so choose one that's washable. While you're washing the spread, you may want to dye it as well. Follow dye package instructions and, for ease, do it in the washing machine.

Old and new quilts have been used as bedspreads for decades. Gwen made one for her bed. If you add lace over a solid-colored bedspread or sheet, you'll achieve a very pretty country look. If you crochet, you can make a bedspread or a topper. A lace tablecloth does the job of a topper too. A small lace or Battenburg-edged table cloth placed on top of a bedspread or comforter adds the look of a lace cover inexpensively. It can be sewn onto the bedspread or just spread over the top.

If the comforter you own is not to your liking, change its appearance quickly by making a duvet cover. A duvet is like a huge pillowcase that fits over your comforter. It also protects the comforter from soiling. You can whip off a duvet cover and wash it quickly. You can even have a couple of duvets to change the look of your bed quickly.

To make a duvet, take two sheets (that are the right size), place the right sides together, and stitch around the edges. Leave the foot end open so you can put the comforter inside. Close it with buttons, Velcro, or ties made of ribbon or leftover sheet fabric. Only the top sheet needs to be seen unless you want to make the cover reversible. You may want to make the lining in a coordinating fabric so that the underside looks coordinated when turned back. If you will only be seeing the top, a less expensive sheet can be used for the underside. Duvet covers are available at linen stores, some department stores, and sometimes at shoestring places. Watch for sales.

Piles of pretty fringed pillows on the bed will add a sumptuous look and come in handy when you want to prop yourself up to read in bed. These extra pillows can provide a way to repeat a pattern, print, or color that needs repeating in a room. (Remember—always have at least three places for any pattern, color, or motif you introduce into a room.)

If you want a romantic mood in the master bedroom, create it by using lots of white or pastels, lace, flowers, and candles. Be generous with fabric on the bed, windows, and tables. Pile a mound of pretty pillows on the bed. Finish it all off with special touches, including prettily framed photos on a table, floral prints on the walls, and accessories made of silver, crystal, or glass.

Restful color schemes give a feeling of peace, tranquillity, and luxury. Bright, primary colors and jarring contrasts are not restful to the eye or the spirit. Monochromatic color schemes in pastels, white, creams, or grays are great for creating a restful feel. Using the same print throughout the room is another easy way to bring peace and continuity to a room and to make a small room seem bigger.

Traditional

Let's play with a monochromatic color scheme for our traditional style. (NOTE: There are some ideas here that could also be used in a contemporary master bedroom.) Using a monochromatic scheme is an easy way to decorate because there is no color matching. The key to successful one-color schemes is to use a mixture of rich textures throughout the room.

Let's use the neutral color of tan for our example (any neutral will work). The wood furniture for this room can be any wood tone you like, but try for at least very similar, if not matching, wood tones throughout. You may need to strip and restain some pieces to achieve a unified color.

Say you are the proud owner of a tan damask bedspread, which inspired the room's color in the first place. Take down your white curtains (supposing that's what you have) and gather up any other white, washable fabric items in the room, and wash them using about sixteen tea bags to a tub of hot water. Soak the fabric in the tea until they reach the color you want. The result will be a lovely antique tan. (Before you begin dyeing, you might first experiment on white rags to see if this is the color and effect you want.)

Add tan fringe or trim to edges of curtains and some of the other items to give them more texture and detail. Make tan slipcovers for upholstered seating using canvas or thick fabric drop cloths. Add trims, fringes, piping, and tassels to these as well.

Take two ceramic lamps that are about the same size, and use craft paints (that are found in craft stores to be used on glass and ceramic) to paint the lamp bases tan, then add a marble effect with a marbling kit. Choose lamp shades of white or tan. Make "skirts" for the lamp shades with ribbon and bows at the "waist." (Described earlier in chapter 8.)

Another quick way to change the appearance of a lamp is to make a covering that is shaped like a pillowcase and slip it over the base. Tie it at the "waist" with a ribbon and bow. Experiment a little to see if you want to line the pillowcase so that a contrasting color shows when the top gathered edge of the covering turns back. Gwen took a one-dollar thrift store lamp in good working order and slipcovered it to match her decor. A plain white shade with a band of trim at the top and bottom (glued on) completes the look.

Go to your thrift stores and think white or tan. Look for fabrics of different textures in these colors, such as old, nubby bedspreads, chenille robes or spreads, damasks, laces, and silky things. Visit your fabric store and look for price-reduced remnants. Dye the white things tan. Use these bits and pieces to make pillows, top a table, make a chair pad, cover a lamp shade, make tiebacks, and cover boxes. Use them any place fabric is used. The idea is to add rich textures, details, and interest by using many materials of about the same color. Be generous with ruffles if that is your style. Add ribbon, tassels, fringes, or other trim where you can.

Including some shiny traditional accessories will add traditional elegance. Use silky fabrics, shiny brass candlesticks, cut glass, and ceramics. You might also include silver or gold frames, a collection of figurines, a glass vase filled with flowers, and perfume bottles. Marble can be tan, so marbleize a tabletop with tan tones and then protect it with a couple of coats of glossy polyurethane finish.

Art objects really stand out in this scheme, so here is a good place to show them off. The room can become a backdrop for displaying a unique sculpture on a pedestal. Wall art or a wonderful rug will show to best advantage in your monochromatic room. Your wood furniture will also add contrast and look sculptural. To give texture to the walls, sponge or rag roll two or three different shades of light tans onto them.

It is, as always, the details that provide the traditional master bedroom with that decorator's touch. Your personal collection of nicely framed photos on a tabletop, pretty things like perfume bottles, vases of flowers, a silver comb, brush, and mirror set, an old christening gown hung on a screen or on the back of a door, a tray with tea things, a few old books stacked on a table, the ever-present alarm clock, mirrors, and other wall art are all important details in creating your style. Display these things if they have the look of quality and fit in with your decorating plan.

Country

Country decor can begin with lots of things: a hooked or braided rug, antique pictures, a handmade dresser scarf, or an old quilt. Let's say you have a nice old quilt that Aunt Martha gave you. There are a couple of things you can do with it. You can hang it on the wall or use it as a bedspread. Let's suppose that the most prominent color in the quilt is mint green. Off you go to the paint store carrying your quilt (or you might bring paint chips home so that you can see what the paint will look like in the light in your country bedroom). Now ask yourself if you want a matching green or if you would prefer to go a bit lighter or darker. Let's say you paint the walls a medium mint green and then sponge on a lighter mint green for texture and contrast. Use white on trim and woodwork in the room. Use white linens—maybe with a mint green trim sewn on—a white lamp shade and some small photos framed in white. Hang some country-look wall art, perhaps in frames you've found at a thrift store and painted white. Add some mint green trim to white pillows. Find a white and mint green print to use for a table topper, a pillow, or tiebacks. You have just created a showstopping country room.

If your furniture isn't fine old antiques or nice new wood, paint it all white. This is an easy way to take all those pieces of furniture you purchased at yard sales and thrift stores in all those different wood tones and styles and give them unity. Besides, it's very trendy.

A country room wouldn't be complete without a generous amount of flowers. A picnic bench at the foot of the bed will look like folk art and bring a hint of the garden into your country bedroom. Top the bench with a print cushion for comfort and color. Remember to add some of the usual country touches: baskets, folk art, lace, and ruffles.

Contemporary

For a comfortable master bedroom with contemporary style, follow the advice above to achieve a monochromatic color scheme. Instead of tassels and bows, though, use piping and flat ribbon for trims. Keep clutter to a minimum. Use modern art.

Furniture in a contemporary bedroom will have clean, graceful lines. Natural wood finishes bring out the sculptural beauty of the fine workmanship that often characterizes contemporary furniture. You will also find beds made of metals to complement the look.

Your master bedroom may not be big enough to use all these great ideas for vanities, reading corners, and such. That's OK. Use what you can to create a comfortable oasis, a retreat—a peaceful, comfortable refuge to look forward to at the end of the day.

CHAPTER 15

Kids' Rooms

Enter at Your Own Risk!

Kids rooms are such fun places to decorate. Here you can let your creativity go wild. You can create a cowboy's haven, a race car driver's pit stop, a ballerina's backstage retreat, or a castle for a princess.

An important consideration in decorating these rooms is to keep in mind the little people who will be using them. Is the room easy to clean? Or will all those curtains in the princess's bedroom collect so much dust that the princess is constantly sneezing? Is that light-colored carpet in your boys' rooms going to show bits of smashed crayons or model airplane paint? Or could you find a speckled tweed rug that hides it all?

Once again, it's time to think before picking up a paintbrush—about how these rooms should function, the likes and dislikes of those who live in them, and making these rooms easy for the occupants to care for on their own.

The Nursery

Decorating a nursery, especially for the first time, is lots of fun. Women find all those cute prints and pastel colors irresistible. Often a lot of effort goes into creating a luxurious nursery. The movie *Father of The Bride II* epitomizes the extreme possibilities. The fictional characters added a huge room to their home and decorated it lavishly for the baby to come. It was funny in a movie, but we're pretty sure that isn't the best use of your shoestring resources. Remember, the baby stage doesn't last long. When planning the nursery, it is wise to consider the needs of all the stages that follow babyhood. Think about adaptability and changeability when you invest in furnishings.

Often a young mother-to-be knows if she is preparing for a girl or a boy and that will affect her decisions about colors and decorating. If she doesn't know the sex of her baby, or chooses not to know, a decorating scheme that will work for either a boy or girl is a good idea.

Jo's first nursery was a large, sunny room. It being the good old days, she didn't know the sex of the baby. Someone made her a baby quilt that was mostly yellow with some brown in it. It was too pretty to use, so she hung it on the wall and let it dictate the color scheme for the room.

Often family and friends want to give baby items to a couple having their first child. Don't be embarrassed; allow people to help you at this important time of your life. Gwen remembers that an uncle gave her a very good crib that she used for both of her children. Someone else gave her a wardrobe that had drawers and doors. She painted those two pieces yellow. The church where she and her husband were assistant pastors gave them a rocking chair.

If you sew, check the pattern books in fabric stores. They are full of ideas and patterns to sew up an adorable nursery. If you are like most of us, you will be combining things on loan from friends with things you buy yourself. Tying it all together can be a challenge.

Items such as a crib or cradle don't easily wear out, and if they are in good condition and safe, many families can use them. If no one is lending or handing these items down, you can usually find baby furniture at yard sales. Go early because pieces sell fast.

Generally, you cannot paint or refinish a friend's possession, so if you plan to have several children, you might prefer your own baby furnishings. Almost every town now has a consignment shop where you can buy used baby furniture. Regular shoestring places have baby furniture too. Also watch the classifieds. Just be sure that what you purchase is safe. Go to a baby department in a regular store and check out the cribs before purchasing one second-hand. This will benefit you in two ways. You can read the tag on the crib and talk with the clerk about crib safety. And the prices of new cribs will encourage you to try a shoestring alternative!

Remember, you don't have to start with every piece of furniture in a nursery. One of Jo's girlfriends was putting her husband through medical school when baby number one was on the way. They were short on money and space. They used a nice playpen for the crib. Later it did double duty as a playpen.

You can take a decorating cue from things you already plan to use in the room, like a wall hanging or rug. If you are starting from scratch, choose an ensemble at a store, and let all your friends know what you've chosen so they can buy something you really want at baby shower time. You can take a motif from the linens you choose and stencil a border at chair rail height. Tie in a design from wallpaper by stenciling the design on a wooden valance, painted furniture, or anywhere else that pleases you.

Keep wall borders at a height where the little one can appreciate it. A chair rail will meet the eye of the baby in the crib and on the changing table. A large border at the bottom of the walls will delight a crawling or toddling baby. Coloring books, bed linens, posters, and storybooks are inexpensive sources of simple designs. Use a copier to shrink or expand the design to the desired size. Then use carbon paper to transfer the design to the surface being painted. Use paintbrushes and paint pens found in craft stores to fill in the design with color. Glossy paints look more cheerful than flat-based paints and are more durable and easy to clean. Finally, protect your designs and artwork with a couple coats of polyurethane.

Whatever you decide to use to decorate your baby's nursery, make it washable because it *will* get dirty! Things like wallpaper and paint will look pretty sad and worn in just a few years because of the hard use a little one can give them. But things like window blinds, flooring, and light fixtures will last a long time, so make them more neutral. You can still use them when you change from baby blue bunnies to big boy baseball designs. Furniture will be your most enduring acquisition. You will want to use the large pieces like dressers and storage units during all the stages of your child's growing up years. Al and Jo are still using dressers their parents bought for their childhood bedrooms decades ago.

A basic rule of thumb for the nursery: Don't buy more than you need. Think your purchases through carefully because you can easily spend too much money.

Color

Consider carefully the colors you use for the nursery. Do you want a stimulating room with lots of bright colors? Or do you want a quiet and peaceful room more suited to sleeping? Determine the functions and needs of the room. You may want to save the bright colors for a playroom, den, or family room, where the child will be spending his waking hours and getting stimulation not only from colors, but also from the rest of the family.

The color and the design you choose may have to last a long time. How often do you plan to redecorate this room? If redecorating will be several years down the road, you may want to use solid colors, stripes, or gingham checks that will still look appropriate when the child is older. Paint and strippable borders are easy to redo, but you may not want to very often because of the cost and time involved!

Window treatments can be anything that is safe for the child. Simple shades or blinds will darken a room so baby will sleep better and may even sleep past sunrise later on. (Daylight wakens most people and almost all toddlers!) A pretty valance and curtains to frame the window can carry out the theme of the room.

When you have a baby, all kinds of gross things can end up on the floor. So why do we usually put down carpeting in the nursery? Yes, it is warm and quiet, but it will get soiled. This is a good place for a really cheap, washable rug to protect the carpet. (For safety's sake, use carpet tape around the rug's perimeter to make sure it doesn't turn up at the edges or slide.)

Later when baby becomes a toddler, he or she will spend a lot of playing time on the floor. If the nursery will also be his playroom, flooring that is easy to clean makes sense. Kids will need a smooth surface to run cars and trucks and set up action figures. Jo often had to roll up the rug in her two boys' playroom to give them more space on the wooden floor to do their "driving." A smooth floor also works better as a foundation for their building blocks, Lincoln Logs, and Legos.

Let's play with a few ideas for the nursery that will carry through to later years.

Country Gingham Nursery

Gingham is a versatile and fun fabric for decorating. Fabric stores carry many colors and sizes. Linen stores carry bed linens and accessories in gingham prints. It is a classic country cottage look. Choose gingham in one or two complementary colors, with one dominating, and cover everything with them. (Or use the same color gingham in all the different size checks you find.) Make curtains, sheets, pad covers, table clothes, chair pads, quilts, diaper holder, lamp shade skirts, and stuffed toys. Apply white rickrack trim to hems. Paint the furniture white. Paint the lower half of the room the color of the gingham. Add a border that uses the same color at chair-rail height. Paint the upper half of the room in stripes in the same color.

Baby Boy's Room

A little boy may enjoy a blue nursery with cars and trucks as a design theme. Begin with a clean background of white walls and white curtains.

Buy or make a large stencil of cars and trucks. Use it at the hems of your curtains or valances. Use primary colors, emphasizing blue.

Sponge blue paint on the ceiling and the upper eighteen inches of the walls to make blue skies. On the white walls below, spatter on the three primary colors evenly. Stencil on a two-inch wide red border stripe where the blue meets the white walls.

At floor level, stencil big twelve- to eighteen-inch cars and trucks on the walls, all around the room. Include road signs here and there.

Paint furniture and shelves white. Add blue to the edges. Choose storage bins for toys in white and primary colors. Plan ahead how many, what colors, and what sizes of containers you need before going shopping. Construct and paint wooden boxes to hold toys. Make them light enough that your little one will be able to help at cleanup time.

Choose linens in solid or striped blue-and-white. Later when he is using a real bed, find blue linens printed with cars and trucks.

Display a collection of cars and trucks on shelves. Rugs with city streets printed on them are available for little boys to drive their Matchbox cars on. Fabric with the same idea is available so you can make your own floor cloth for junior to drive on. Or you can paint a canvas floor cloth with the same design.

Baby Girl's Room

We have to begin with the classic baby girl color—pink, of course. Let's play with that naughty bunny that Beatrix Potter brought to life, Peter Rabbit, and the irresistible garden of Mr. McGregor. Once again we will begin with a clean slate of white walls and white curtains.

Paint the upper half of the walls soft pink. Use a chair rail border with a rabbit or gardening theme. Or for fun, paint a clothesline on the wall with tiny rabbit clothing hanging out to dry. Paint a garden scene on the lower half of the wall. Include vegetables, flowers, watering cans, gardening tools, clay flowerpots, and of course Peter Rabbit in the garden with a white picket fence in the background. Leave behind his shoes, hat, and coat here and there. (Don't be intimidated by the idea of painting on the walls. Remember you can enlarge drawings from books and transfer the designs to the walls with carbon paper. Use a book's pictures to guide you in painting the figures so they look like they are supposed to look.)

Display stuffed rabbits throughout the room. (Shoestringers will buy them right after Easter at discount store closeouts.) Tie big pink bows around their necks. Use clay flowerpots for storing things on shelves.

Add a band of inch-wide pink ribbon to the edges of the white curtains. Finish off the lampshade edges with a thin row of pink braid. For linens, use pink-and-white solids and dots. Add big pink bows wherever you can.

Hang pictures on the walls of gardens and bunnies, nicely matted with gold frames. Leave furniture its natural wood color.

On dresser tops, use white tablecloths with pink bands of ribbons sewn one-inch from the hems.

The charm of this room will last for years. When your young lady gets tired of living with rabbits, a coat or two of paint will cause them to disappear.

Here's a tip: Chenille is back in full force. Use it in a baby's room for crib bumpers, teddy bears, quilts and crib covers, and even lamp shades. Use different woven patterns and a different patchwork of colors for each item. Use pastel pink, yellow, blue, mint green, and white.

Kids' Bedroom

Kid's bedrooms usually do double duty as playrooms. This arrangement can be a bit crowded and messy, so we need to discuss storage and organizational ideas.

Manufacturers have finally figured out that we have a lot of stuff that needs storing and organizing. (We've never heard of a kid who got less and less stuff as the years rolled on.) There are now many types of bins, tubs, baskets, and other products to help you get a handle on organizing your children's things. Invest in large furniture-type storage pieces to which you can add more units. Get the sturdiest units possible because the kids use them to play in, stand on, and for other imaginative play. Use a color that will go with any redecorating that may come up in the next few years.

Many people use the old idea of a toy box. This makes it easy to clean up because everything goes in one spot. But a child will inevitably want the toy at the bottom, so he'll empty it every time. What a mess! If you do opt for a toy box, make sure it has a safety catch so the lid will not fall on the child and do serious harm. It should not have a lock, so if the child hides in there he can escape.

Stuffed animals seem to multiply. They can go on the bed, but that can get to be a bit too much to deal with every day—off, on; off, on. Consider using a net, hung like a hammock in the corner of a room to hold toys. A shelf one or two feet from the ceiling all around the room can show off and store stuffed animals that are currently not being tucked in with the child. Any other "treasures" the child receives that are not really meant to be played with, plus some framed photos of Mom and Dad, can go on the shelf as well.

Decorating a kid's room can be a lot of fun. They have definite ideas about colors and themes, so let them tell you what they like, and then you can have the fun making it work. There is no limit to what you can do with a little paint and creativity.

For the Sports Nut

There are comforters, bed linens, borders, and posters galore for almost every major league team. These are expensive—unless you get them on sale—but fun. For more generic decorating, you can find a comforter that uses the main colors in many sports pennants and posters. Jo has found that most of her sons' baseball pennants and posters have navy blue and white on them. Jo painted the room white with navy blue trim to pull it all together. Their comforters are navy blue, also.

A long shelf along the wall near the ceiling, bookshelves, headboards with shelves, and a dresser top work for showing off trophies and sports-related objects. Like stuffed animals, these also multiply, so plan for more display space than you think you will ever need.

A golf club or baseball bat can function as a curtain rod. Pennants hung points down over the top of a window work as a valance. A row of pennants tacked up end to end two feet below the ceiling make a border. Stencil horizontal lines just above and below the pennants to give the whole treatment a finished look.

There are also many nice sports-related wallpaper borders available. Team them with a striped or solid wall for a snazzy look. Or paint the top one foot of the walls to match the ceiling. Below that put a sports border and below that a solid or striped paint job.

An old, recycled locker in a corner or a short one as a bed-side table fits the theme and provides more storage. If you have a jersey or T-shirt from your child's earlier playing days, have it framed and hang it on the wall.

For a Camping Theme

Rig up a piece of canvas to look like the opening of a tent for a headboard. Use green and brown as a color scheme throughout the room. Find a plaid blanket or comforter with those colors to cover the bed.

Get more of the camping theme into the room with canvas tab curtains or a forest print for curtains. Hang curtains over a fishing pole or bring in a branch and turn it into a curtain rod. Paint some evergreen trees in a corner or even all along one wall. Paint underbrush and pinecones at the bottom of the wall, just above the baseboard.

An alternative idea for the walls is to use a wallpaper or paint treatment to make the walls look like they are made of logs or wood planks. Make it look like a woodsy cabin. Display stuffed bears in corners, on shelves, and on the bed. A camping stool and table can be used as a desk.

Pine cones and fir branches can be stenciled on lamp shades and elsewhere. See what camping gear you have around that can be used for daily needs and decoration. Put a fake bear rug on the floor. Make a clothes tree for your child to hang clothes on by choosing a real tree branch that has thick limbs. Cut the limbs short—about two to four inches in length. Anchor the tree branch in a bucket or keg filled with small stones.

A Fairy Tale Theme

Have fun with this theme. Paint or construct a wooden fairy tale castle as a headboard. Cover the bed with a solid pastel comforter—a very popular idea right now.

Over window blinds, for light control and privacy, layer curtains of sheers made of tulle, dotted-Swiss, or some other filmy fabric like a princess would wear. Pull the curtains back with a tiara or string of gaudy beads. Stencil stars on the sheers for a fairy-tale look.

Trace and paint or stencil fairy-tale characters along the bottom of a wall, at the lowest level possible. (Add grass for your figures to walk on!) For a border about one foot from the ceiling or at chair rail height, paint or stencil the beginning lines of a fairy tale, in five- or six-inch-tall letters ("Once upon a time, in a land far, far away, there lived a beautiful princess and a . . .")

In wallpaper books, you will find borders and wallpapers in every imaginable fairy-tale theme. You may want to invest in these or merely use one for inspiration. Use a storybook or coloring book to get figures to copy for stenciling and painting.

How to Enlarge a Picture for Painting on a Wall

The simpler the picture, the easier this will be. That's why coloring and comic books make good patterns.

1. Make a copy of the picture on a copy machine. (We will be using the copy, not the original, to work with.) You need to decide how big the picture will be on the wall (three feet? ten feet?). Enlarge the picture to one-twelfth the size of the completed wall picture (e.g., one inch equals one foot).
2. Make little marks, one inch apart, all the way around the pattern picture. Connect the dots with lines to make a one-inch grid over the entire picture. (See illustration 15.1.)
3. Very lightly track a similar grid on the wall you want to decorate. This time the lines will be one foot apart.
4. Beginning at the top left corner of the picture's grid and the corresponding corner of the wall's grid, draw with a pencil what is in that square onto the wall. Go square by square until the whole pattern has been transferred onto the wall.
5. Paint the picture onto the wall in the colors you have chosen. Cover your art with a coat or two of polyurethane so all that your artistic work will last a long time.

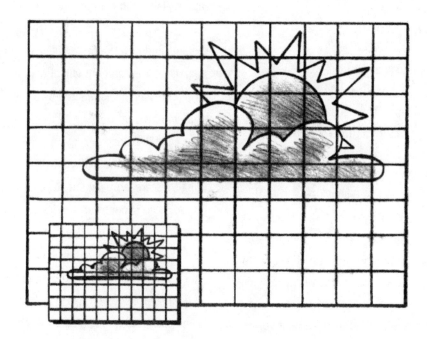

Illustration 15.1
Enlarging pictures on a wall diagram

Dinosaur Theme

There are ready-made fabrics and wallpapers with dinosaurs, but you only need them for inspiration. There are plenty of coloring and other books about these big fascinating creatures. Lift ideas for stenciling and painting from them. Paint one or two huge dinosaurs on the walls. Paint a row of them along the floor all around the room. Make them big! Add some trees for them to eat. Paint some flying dinosaurs on the sky-ceiling. Have plenty of stuffed dinos around. (There are patterns for making them, and you can choose colors that fit whatever color scheme you've chosen.) You can stencil them everywhere, of course. To let the focus be on the dinosaurs, use solid colors on the windows and beds.

Teens' Rooms

Decorating a teen's room may be a questionable venture! Your teen certainly needs to be consulted and involved with all the decisions, shopping, and work. The needs, tastes, and desires of a teen are vastly different from those of a child. Now your teen is pulling away from you and establishing his own ideas about everything. Letting your teen have a choice about his room is a good, safe way to let him try his wings.

We realize that many teens simply do not want their rooms "decorated." But they may be amenable to a new bedspread and a fresh coat of paint. Honor their wishes and close the door to their rooms, if you need to. The relationship with your teen is much more important than a room's decor.

But if your teen is interested in creating a pleasant space, be sure to have the teen go through an evaluation process to decide just exactly what he wants, how he wants it to function, and exactly how she wants it to look. Some teens use their rooms as private dens where they entertain their friends. Some like to have their own music and entertainment there. Some may want to have the bedroom be a place where no one bothers them or their precious stuff. They may need a desk and computer. Think it through thoroughly.

Your teen may be ready for a more grown-up look. As with every room you plan to redo, both you and your teen may want to look through magazines and decorating books and note what catches the eye. Do not just look at bedrooms. Inspiration could come from anywhere: dens, living rooms, and family rooms. After looking at a few books, your teen may decide on a country or traditional look. He may want his room to resemble an English library. So do the research first! This may be the time to begin investing in furnishings that will get him through college and into the first few years of his career and even early marriage. Your student will always need a desk, a chair, a bed, and a dresser. Investing in new or used pieces of good quality that will hold up through all these stages and the many moves that will take place during this time makes a lot of sense and will cost less in the long run. Other things that may be used a long time are lamps, good rugs, mirrors, clocks, and storage units. So consider your purchases carefully.

The need for storage doesn't go away when kids become teens. It may be time to ruthlessly go through all toys and junk and clean things out to make room for new acquisitions. Box up and store precious things; give away the rest. This provides a clean slate and more space to work with. As a teen becomes an adult, the shelves and other storage units will be needed to accommodate his new interests and needs.

Use as much from the previous decorating scheme as you can. Paint and dyes can transform most things. Your only expenses may be for paint and new wall borders.

Need ideas to get you and your teen inspired? Here are a few:

Contemporary

For a sophisticated, contemporary look, black-and-white is a good choice. Paint the bed and other furniture a glossy black. Walls will be white. You can stick with solid white for curtains and bedspreads or go with a flashy print that has black-and-white in it on the bed, for a border on the walls, and for the curtains. With this simple but striking look, judiciously choose only a couple of posters or prints for the wall, simply framed in silver or black. The less clutter the better. If all the accessories are black, white, and one of the colors chosen from a print you use, the room will look unified and together. Simple miniblinds in black or white, with or without a valance, will give it a streamlined look.

Horses

If your teen is a horse nut, she probably already owns horse posters, pictures, and statuary. Any nicely framed photos of your teen with a horse and other well-framed pictures of horses will be displayed on walls and elsewhere. Choose a border for the walls of horses, horseshoes, or country scenes that evoke images of a ride in the country. Choose a color scheme that matches a favorite horse, then add blue or green to give an outdoor feel to the room. Solids and plaids will add to the horsey, country feeling.

Music

There are some clever wallpapers and borders with music symbols. You can make your own too. Use old sheet music or copies of it to cover a wall or use as a border. Use wallpaper glue to affix it to the wall. Cut a sponge to look like a quarter note and randomly paint notes all over the walls A stencil would also work for this.

There are fabrics with musical themes to use for curtains and duvets, or you can create your own with those sponges and stencils on a plain background. Posters with musical themes or advertising musical events will go on the walls (nicely framed, of course). The musical instrument of choice with a music stand can fill in a corner. Perhaps a collection of antique or miniature musical instruments will be displayed somewhere. Christmas tree ornaments in the shapes of instruments and musical notes can adorn curtain rods and tiebacks, hang on bedposts or a lamp, or hang on the end of the chain that dangles from a ceiling fan. Plastic note ornaments are flat, so they can be glued in a row around a lamp shade, along the top edge of a headboard, around a mirror, or on the back of a chair.

Nature

Paint a mural of a forest or some other nature scene on one, or even all, of the walls. Use natural colors of browns and greens. Paint the ceiling sky blue. Use posters from the forest service and frame them. Collections of miniature animals, birds' nests, rocks, dried flowers, or pine cones can be displayed. Simple tab curtains hung on a branch works for the windows. Affix pine cones or tiny two-inch teddy bears found at a craft store to the ends for finials.

Use furniture in natural wood finishes. It should have a rustic feel to it. Create a twig headboard. Use wicker, wooden boxes, and baskets for storage. Add some real or silk flowers in rustic clay pots, wooden boxes, baskets, or small tin buckets to the window sill. Choose a favorite plant or animal from nature, and use its silhouette or likeness throughout the room.

Masculine

Browns, black, gray, and deep green are considered manly colors. Rough, nubby textures, leather, metallic looks, and wood are also masculine. Keep the room unfussy, using plaids or stripes. Details could include brass touches, evidences of any manly pursuits such as golf or hunting, trophies, books, and most anything in leather or wood.

Feminine

Conversely, your teenage girl may want a very feminine room with all the lace, pastels, florals, ribbons, and bows she can get. Cover the bed with a floral bedspread, grace the windows with ruffles or lace, and paint the walls in a sweet coordinating pastel. Paint all the trim and furniture white. A canopy bed and skirted vanity would add even more feminity. On the wall, hang some gold-framed botanical or romantic scenes. Display collections of pretty tea sets, dolls, china figurines, or other feminine touches.

Shoestring Tips

- Think about longevity with colors and furniture.
- Bookshelves full of books encourage reading. Make sure there is a comfortable place to read with adequate lighting.
- Ceiling fans will cool a room and can be found in many styles.
- Little girls may want a vanity and a corner set aside for doll play.
- Bunk beds provide twice the sleeping space for the same space as a twin bed and later can be "debunked."
- Let your child help with painting, sponging, and the other work involved with redecorating his or her room.
- Find posters for walls in magazines and newspapers.
- Other theme ideas: jungle, castle, nautical, garden, Victorian, any sport, dance, a cartoon, Star Wars, Star Trek, money, animals, a movie, under the sea, submarines, travel, space, old western town, career, farm, zoo, prehistoric age, arctic, dessert, downtown, cave, construction site, art, hot air balloons, theater, clubhouse, tree house, ranch, airport, airplanes, trains, sunflowers, kitchen, gas station, beauty shop, Legos, a branch of the armed forces, hunting, safari, Sesame Street, a kids' television show, cliff dwelling, futuristic city, ski slope, and geology.

CHAPTER 16

Little Things Mean a Lot

We've covered a lot of ground in these pages! By now, your head is probably spinning with many ideas for decorating your home without spending a fortune. Shoestring decorating is a lifestyle choice, one that we believe you will find rewarding. There's so much more we could explore on this subject. However, once you're started, you'll discover many fresh ideas yourself.

There are lots of little inexpensive touches that can add your personality and style to your home. Anyone can add these little niceties and turn plain into wonderful! While working on this book, Gwen accepted a new job and had to move to a temporary apartment 120 miles away. It was the middle of a bleak Michigan winter, so she gathered up every flowered, pretty thing she had and loaded them into the moving van. She brought birdhouses, dried floral wreaths and pictures, lacy curtains, and white painted furniture to dress up her little one-bedroom apartment. She brought one big armoire to hold her TV and stereo system, and three bookcases to hold her books.

These are the things that bring her comfort. By surrounding herself with books and music, she made her temporary abode a livable place.

We encourage everyone—singles as well as couples—to begin today making your house a home. Start making a place special the first day you move into a new dwelling. Put up some pretty towels, put some fresh flowers in a favorite vase on the kitchen table, throw some pretty decorative pillows on a bed, and light a candle. For each of us, the little touches that make a house a home are slightly different. Let's take a walk through a house and think about ideas that will add those little touches to your home.

Front Porch or Entryway

The front door, doorbell, welcome mat, and front outside light all say something about you. You might ask yourself what your front entryway says about you. Keep things clean. It doesn't cost a cent, and it is the best decorating advice we can give you.

More and more new houses have front porches, and they are wonderful places to begin adding personal touches. Hang lanterns, lights, baskets of flowers, wind chimes, or other decorative items.

Look for unusual containers for potted flowers. Gwen uses cachepots she found sitting by the roadside when a neighbor moved out of her house, and a coal scuttle she picked up at a dump many years ago. You can use watering cans, wooden crates, and large terra cotta pots (often available at thrift shops, especially off-season) to hold flowers. Add an antique milk can painted and topped with a plant or filled with walking sticks.

Provide seating outside your front door. Gwen's neighbors have a cut-down church pew on the porch. Gwen had her brother make a special bench that fits her own porch perfectly.

Think of your front porch and doorstep as an introduction to the rest of your home. You can introduce your indoor theme here. Think, too, of how this area will be used. If you have a porch, what time of the day will you sit there? What do you need to make family members comfortable? Rocking chairs, wrought-iron furniture, Adirondack chairs, retro metal chairs, or wicker? If you plan to sit on your porch, make sure there is place to put down a cup, glass, or snack.

Put a nice sturdy welcome mat at the doorway. A high-quality, plain sisal mat probably does the best job. To create a designer style mat, try stenciling on a design using spray paint.

Keep the lawn clutter-free, green, and trimmed. Flowers in a pot by the front door give a cheerful welcome during spring and summer months. Sweep the front walk and porch. Brush cobwebs away from the door and porch area as well. Keep the front door clean. Have an attractive porch light and large house numbers near the front door that can be seen easily from the street. Display seasonal wreaths and other decorations on the outside of the door.

Now let's open the front door and go in.

Foyer

We've already talked about the importance of this area in welcoming friends and family. So now, let's just talk about little touches.

The foyer usually includes a guest coat closet. Clean out extra coats. Put some pretty hat boxes on the shelves to store mittens, gloves, and scarves. Buy some padded hangers in colors that match the hat boxes. (Gwen has found lots of padded hangers at thrift shops for about fifty cents each.) If your closet has a door that opens out, put a mirror on the back of the door so that your guests can take a quick peek at themselves when they are coming or going. You can even paper or paint your closet to match or contrast with the rest of the foyer. Add a battery-powered closet light for convenience.

An umbrella stand is a nice touch. What you use doesn't have to be a real umbrella stand. You can use any tall, thin cylinder: a tall vase in your room's colors, a coal scuttle, an old milk can, a decorative metal garbage can, or anything your eye spots when you learn to keep it open and your mind working on new ideas for old objects.

If there's room, add a small bench where family members can sit to put on and remove outdoor footwear. If you don't have a closet, get a good coat tree, or put up some decorative hooks for hanging guests' coats. You may have room for a small hall table, a mirror, and flowers or candles that will say "welcome" to your family and guests. Mirrors bring light and visually expand the size of a dark hallway or foyer. Keep clutter, shoes, and other things cleared away. You will also need a rug on which to wipe feet and to define this space.

First impressions of your home also include the way it smells. Does your home have an unpleasant odor? Ask a friend to give you an honest opinion, because our noses become so accustomed to our daily smells that we no longer notice them. Fresh air helps. Whenever possible, open the windows of your home to air it out. A lovely container of potpourri and scented candles near the front door offer a pleasant, welcoming scent. Before company arrives, put a cinnamon stick and some cloves in an open saucepan with water and boil it for a few minutes. You can also use a scent ring. This is a small circular device that fits on the top of a lamp's bulb. Put a few drops of fragrant oil on the ring, and the heat from the bulb will send the fragrance into the air. Be sure you don't mix fragrances in the house. One scent is enough.

Do everything you can to make the entryway of your home a special place of greeting.

Living Room

This is probably the place where you will entertain guests. Make it special with little touches. The coffee or tea table in this room is a great place to display lovely picture books, but make sure a book isn't so large that it takes up the entire surface of the table. It needs to be in proportion.

Decorative sofa pillows add much to the decor of the living room and can be changed from time to time to give the room a fresh look. Wonderful coasters are both practical and a nice decorative touch.

Drape a pretty throw over some seating. The room temperature may be just fine for all of your guests but one. It's nice to have a throw available to warm up that guest. Elderly people, especially, need more warmth.

Candles are a relatively inexpensive decorating item. Candles in any room of the house add charm and a sense of warmth. If you have candles in a living room, light them on cool evenings when you have guests. For summer, store candles horizontally, wrapped in tissue.

Gwen once had a friend who was a busy real estate agent. She loved to entertain and said, "I don't always have time to clean, so I just make sure the room is picked up. Then I turn down the lights and light a lot of candles." Not a bad idea if you love company and don't have time to dust and vacuum. Entertaining God's children is a lot more important than a clean house.

Dining Room

This is a place to really think through the little touches that make your home special. Food and eating have always been a way to build relationships through conversation and caring.

Invest in a few good tablecloths and napkins that enhance both the room and your china. Because there are so few people who entertain graciously anymore, you can find wonderful tablecloths in shoestring places. If you find a really wonderful tablecloth dripping with lace or embroidery that is going to require ironing, think about buying it for very special occasions.

The dining room is a great place to use candles—lots of them. Use them on the table singly or in groups. Place votive candles all the way down the center of the table. Use them on a sideboard, in an overhead candelabra, or in wall sconces. The reflected glow of china, flatware, and faces in candlelight is delightful. Make sure that there is enough light that your guests can see what they are eating. Install a dimmer switch to control the exact amount of lighting you want from your chandelier.

If you don't own nice china, you can find it at shoestring places. Remember Jo's china? Half of it came from a garage sale and half from an estate sale. Gwen's good dishes are red-and-white English pottery picked up one piece at a time from thrift shops. She has also purchased one piece at a time a complete set of white fluted dinnerware for everyday use and a set of blue-and-white transfer dinnerware. It's fun to watch for a new and special piece.

Flatware is trickier to find in the usual shoestring places. However, once Gwen found a great big handful of silverplate to match her good set. Perhaps the best way to build a nice set of flatware—stainless or silver—is to pick a pattern and tell family members that's what you want for birthdays and other gift-giving occasions. In the meantime, watch for sales at discount outlets.

We often use a floral centerpiece. Watch shoestring places for interesting and beautiful containers for flowers. A bouquet of fresh flowers in a lovely container has as much appeal as those done by a formal florist and is a lot cheaper. Use garden flowers, leaves, or plants for your arrangements. Gwen enjoys making a bouquet out of just about anything—interesting weeds, branches, greenery, wildflowers. Learn a few tips about arranging cut flowers and buy them at the local grocery store. Remember Jackie Kennedy's White House? She often used simple bouquets of cut flowers at state functions. If she did it, so can we!

Family Room

Family rooms are fun places to add touches that are special to the people you love. Comfy throws, afghans, lots of pillows, and footstools say, "Sit for a while and talk." Shelves full of games and puzzles, favorite books, and toys invite family members to stay awhile and rest.

If you have a library of videos, CDs, or cassette tapes, find a way to keep them easily accessible so they can be enjoyed by the family and hopefully put back where they came from after they've been used.

Bathrooms

In some countries of the world, bathing is almost a ritual. In England bath oils, foaming scented bath products, and wonderful hand-milled soaps are essentials in every bathroom. Big fat towels hung on heated rods nearby are within easy reach.

Make your bathroom a special place for your family or yourself. Keep a scented votive or tea light burning in the powder room or guest bath when entertaining. Put out thick, fluffy towels in the colors of your choice. Better towels last longer and absorb moisture better. Most outlet malls have a linens and bedding store. Watch for closeout bins and sales in those stores.

Get enough hand towels so you can change them often. Whisk wet towels out of the bathroom and into the washer after using one to wipe down fixtures and counters.

Sometimes the only place the mother of a busy family can get away from her family and have some privacy is in the bathroom. Make bathing a special experience. Get yourself some wonderful bath products. A headrest pillow made for the bathtub might be nice. Light some scented votive candles. Draw a bubble bath. Put on some music, climb into the tub, and relax.

If your shower has a glass door, get a shower squeegee and teach your family how to use it. It will prevent lime deposit buildups on the door.

A magazine rack in the bathroom is appreciated by some. An extra mirror so family members can see the back of their heads when grooming would be appreciated. Full-length mirrors either here or in the bedroom are a helpful grooming aid.

Bedrooms

There are so many little touches that make a bedroom a special place. Here are some ideas to give these rooms personality.

Make a pocket that hangs at the side of the bed to hold glasses, a paperback book, a book light, and other items that make your reading time special. A bedside water pitcher and water glass are useful to some.

Family pictures belong in your bedroom either on the wall or in frames clustered on a tabletop. Use flowers—fresh or silk—in your room. Put a favorite piece of art on the wall. In other words, put the things you love most in your own personal space.

Give kids some freedom to decorate their personal spaces. They love posters, floor pillows, sports stuff, and animal items. Little girls love pretty fluff. Let them have what they want in their bedrooms. When they grow up, they'll remember what a happy place home was.

You Can Do This Shoestring Decorating Thing

Once you begin to make decoration a priority, you will find ideas everywhere—in homes you visit, in books, in magazines, at suppliers of home products, and at paint stores, to name a just a few. You, too, can make your home a nicer place to be. Keep a notebook in your purse, and jot down ideas as you come across them. Cut out pictures and file them. Record the names and telephone numbers of people you might need to hire to accomplish your decorating projects.

Home decorating is never really finished. We keep changing, rearranging, adding, subtracting, modifying, improving, and touching up constantly. Things wear out or get faded and tired looking. Sometimes we just get terribly tired of the way things look. Jo keeps a list of projects she wants to do around her home on her desk. Gwen keeps changing houses, so she has ongoing decorating projects, but in different locations. Almost every day both of us do something to slightly improve our homes. It may be as simple as bringing in fresh flowers from the garden, moving pictures around, or putting fresh shelf coverings in the cupboards. By just shifting the position of even small things, you can make your home seem fresh and new. Some people constantly rotate their art and accessories. Some change them seasonally. A slightly more labor-intensive change is to rearrange furniture either within a room or from room to room.

Probably the first, easiest, and cheapest way to begin improving the appearance of your home is to give it a good cleaning, organizing, and decluttering. Get the whole family involved in a blitz. Kids can clean their rooms. Husbands can clean the basement or garage and then give you a hand with the heavy cleaning.

When your house is thoroughly clean, go do some research at your local library. You will find books about every imaginable thing one can do to improve a house. Browse through magazines and books. Walk around craft, fabric, and hardware stores to get inspired and start those creative juices flowing. You will discover many ways to create beauty in your home that we didn't have room to address in this book. New techniques and products are being developed constantly.

While this book narrowed itself primarily to three main styles—traditional, country, and contemporary, (with some mention of combining styles into one eclectic style)—we hope you don't feel confined to only choosing one of these for yourself. We had limits, but you don't! You may find an ethnic, period, regional, national, or other style suits you much better. You'll find our ideas and principles apply to any style.

Be creative! Be you! It is the details, personal touches, and, most importantly, the mood you set that make your home a place where family and friends feel at peace and welcome. Your smile and happiness when greeting a friend or a family member are vastly more important than any decorating you do inside your home. We are, however, confident that if you have stayed with us and are still reading at the end of this book, you now have the tools and inspiration to make your home a lovely place to be. And you, too, can do it all on a shoestring!

A Questionnaire for Determining Your Family's Lifestyle

HOUSE STYLE

What kind of house do you live in?

____Own your own home

____Rent a house

____Apartment

____Condominium or townhouse

____Mobile home

____Other

Do any of them have special needs?____Yes____No

What are those special needs?_____

_____

_____

_____

_____

_____

OCCUPANTS

Who lives in your house?

How many adults?_____

How many children?

Child _____Age_____

Child _____Age_____

Child _____Age_____

Child _____Age_____

Child _____Age_____

Do any of these children have special needs?_____Yes_____No

What are that person(s) needs?

_____

_____

Is there an elderly person living in the home?_____Yes_____No

What are that person(s) needs?

_____

_____

Do you have overnight guests?

_____Frequently_____Rarely_____Never

Our guests

_____become part of the family

_____are treated more formally

LIFESTYLE

What is your basic living style?

_____Casual?

_____Formal?

_____Inexpensive?

_____Luxurious?

_____Quiet?

_____Hectic?

We are homebodies. _____Yes_____No

We are gone a lot. _____Yes_____No

We eat together. _____Yes_____No

Where? (List all the places—patio or porch, family room, etc.)

_____

_____

_____

We eat separately on the run._____Yes_____No

The overall style we prefer is:

_____Traditional

_____Victorian

_____Luxurious

_____Country

_____Theme-related

_____Contemporary

_____High-tech

_____Ethnic

_____Old World

_____Cottage

_____Eclectic

STUDY/WORK

Does someone in this family need office space? A quiet room away from the rest of the family? _____Yes_____No

Does every family member have his own room? If not, where in the house can individuals go to be alone, rest, dream, pursue private activities?

_____

Is a computer used in our home? _____Yes_____No

_____For business

_____To keep track of family records

_____For entertainment

Does someone work from home all the time?

_____Yes_____No

Is there an area for planning, paying bills, menu planning?

_____Yes_____No

Do the children have a place for doing schoolwork?

_____Yes_____No

Do we homeschool?

_____Yes_____No

What kind of facilities do we need to homeschool?

_____

_____

_____

RECREATION/LEISURE

Does the whole family like to be together around some activities?

_____Yes_____No

What are those activities?

_____Listening to stereo

_____Watching TV

_____Playing musical instruments

_____Playing table games or doing puzzles

_____Hobbies or crafts

_____Reading

_____Studying

_____Active indoor play

_____Exercise and aerobic training

_____Active outdoor play or sports

HOBBIES

These are the hobbies of various people in the family and this is the space required for such hobbies:

_____

_____

_____

_____

_____

_____

_____

_____

PETS

These are the kinds of pets we have:

_____

_____

_____

_____

These pets require this kind of space

_____

_____

_____

_____

ENTERTAINING

Our entertaining style is:

_____Formal

_____Casual

_____Large groups

_____Small groups

_____With kids, teenagers

_____Adults only

We entertain in the:

_____Living room

_____Kitchen

_____Family room

_____Dining room

_____Recreation room

_____Outdoors

What is our purpose for entertaining?

_____We entertain primarily for business

_____We entertain socially

The average number of guests is _____

The time of day we usually entertain is_____

We usually entertain at

_____Lunch

_____Buffet supper

_____Formal sit-down dinner

_____Informal sit-down dinner

_____Barbecues, potlucks, and other casual gatherings

For conversation, we prefer:

_____Intimate groups

_____One large group

When eating, we prefer:

_____One large table

_____Several smaller tables

Do we have enough extra seating? _____Yes_____No

COLORS

The Colors We Like Best Are:

_____Muted (Beige/earth tones)

_____Warm (Orange/pink/red)

_____Cool (Blue/green, white)

_____Pastels (pale pink, blue, yellow, green)

_____Sunny (Yellow/gold)

FLOORING

The kinds of floors we like are:

_____Wood

_____Wall to wall carpet

_____Ceramic Tile

_____Brick

_____Vinyl

_____Area rugs over hardwood flooring

LIGHTING

The kind of lighting we like is:

_____Traditional

_____Fan lights

_____Modern

_____Ceiling Lights

_____Antique

_____Table Lamps

_____Floor Lamps

WOODS

The wood tones we prefer are:

Dark_____Light_____Medium_____

Our favorite woods are:

_____Pine

_____Cherry

_____Mahogany

_____Ebony

_____Walnut

_____Birch

_____Maple

_____Other_____

WALLS

We prefer our walls to be:

_____Painted

_____Wallpapered

_____Stenciled

_____Wood Paneled

_____Beadboard

_____Fabric

_____Other_____

FURNISHINGS

Our furniture should be:

_____Modern

_____High-tech (Glass and steel)

_____Rattan, wicker

_____Early American

_____Colonial

_____American Georgian

_____18th-century French

_____Leather

_____Vinyl

_____Marble

_____Fabric

_____Durable

_____Tapestry

_____Luxurious

_____Other_____

WINDOW COVERINGS

We prefer these window treatments:

_____Drapes

_____Modern

_____Period

_____Traditional

_____Country

_____Miniblinds

_____Shutters

_____Balloon or Austrian

_____Valances

_____Lace curtains

_____Cafe

_____Cornices or lambrequins

_____Shades

_____Other_____

ACCESSORIES

For accessories we prefer:

_____Paintings

_____Prints and Lithographs

_____Mirrors

_____Sculptures

_____Antiques

_____Art objects

_____Books

_____Plants

_____Photos

_____Candelabra

_____Plants and dishes

_____Wooden items

_____Country

_____Collections and personal memorabilia

_____Pillows

_____Other_____

FABRICS

The fabrics we prefer are:

_____Tweeds

_____Plaids

_____Country prints

_____Tapestry

_____Chintz

_____Linen

_____Silk

_____Wool

_____Cotton

_____Damask

_____Brocade

_____Velvet

_____Denim

LEISURE

The leisure activities we enjoy which require equipment:

_____Television

_____Videos

_____Audio (CDs, records, tapes, radio)

_____Hot Tub

_____Board and table games

_____Puzzles

_____Gourmet cooking

_____Sports

_____Trains

_____Musical instruments

_____Woodwork and tinkering with mechanical things

_____Gardening

_____Photography

_____Sewing

_____Exercise

Planning Your Furniture Arrangements

After copying these handy template patterns on tracing paper or cutting them out—arrange them on grid paper for an easy way to plan out furniture placement. 1/4" = 1 square foot.

BEDROOM

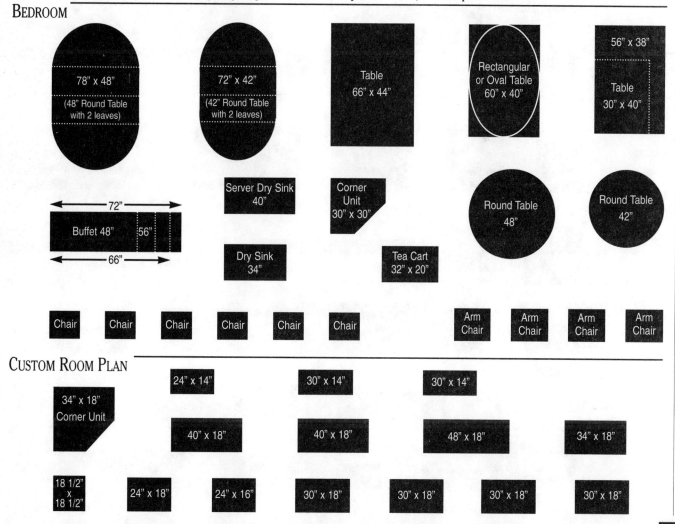

78" x 48"

(48" Round Table with 2 leaves)

72" x 42"

(42" Round Table with 2 leaves)

Table 66" x 44"

Rectangular or Oval Table 60" x 40"

56" x 38"

Table 30" x 40"

72"

Buffet 48"   56"

66"

Server Dry Sink 40"

Corner Unit 30" x 30"

Round Table 48"

Round Table 42"

Dry Sink 34"

Tea Cart 32" x 20"

Chair   Chair   Chair   Chair   Chair   Chair

Arm Chair   Arm Chair   Arm Chair   Arm Chair

CUSTOM ROOM PLAN

24" x 14"

30" x 14"

30" x 14"

34" x 18" Corner Unit

40" x 18"

40" x 18"

48" x 18"

34" x 18"

18 1/2" x 18 1/2"

24" x 18"

24" x 16"

30" x 18"

30" x 18"

30" x 18"

30" x 18"

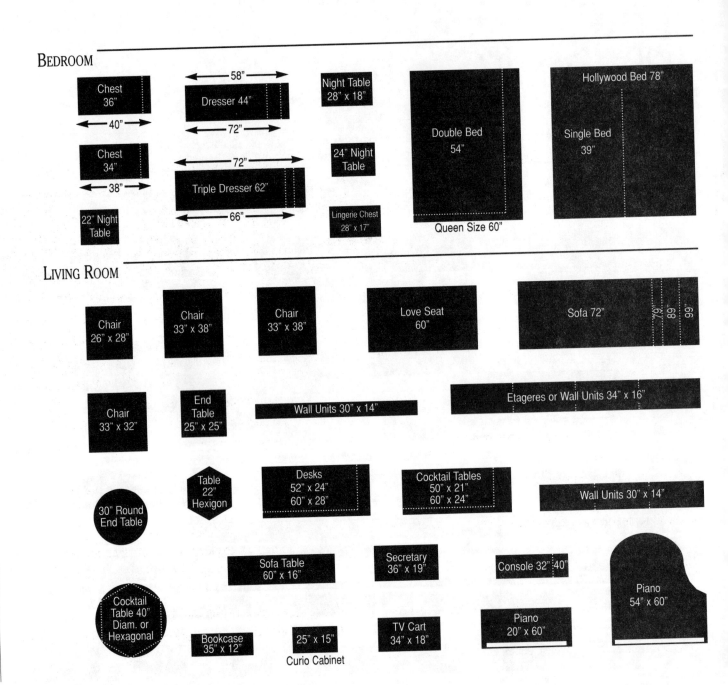

BEDROOM

Chest 36"
← 40" →

Chest 34"
← 38" →

22" Night Table

← 58" →
Dresser 44"
← 72" →

← 72" →
Triple Dresser 62"
← 66" →

Night Table 28" x 18"

24" Night Table

Lingerie Chest 28" x 17"

Double Bed 54"
Queen Size 60"

Hollywood Bed 78"
Single Bed 39"

LIVING ROOM

Chair 26" x 28"

Chair 33" x 38"

Chair 33" x 38"

Love Seat 60"

Sofa 72"
76"
68"
66"

Chair 33" x 32"

End Table 25" x 25"

Wall Units 30" x 14"

Etageres or Wall Units 34" x 16"

30" Round End Table

Table 22" Hexigon

Desks 52" x 24" 60" x 28"

Cocktail Tables 50" x 21" 60" x 24"

Wall Units 30" x 14"

Cocktail Table 40" Diam. or Hexagonal

Sofa Table 60" x 16"

Secretary 36" x 19"

Console 32" 40"

Piano 54" x 60"

Bookcase 35" x 12"

25" x 15"
Curio Cabinet

TV Cart 34" x 18"

Piano 20" x 60"

Glossary

Ambiance: the distinctive atmosphere and feel of your home

Analogous color scheme: groups of three or more colors that are related in hue or are neighbors on the color wheel. (For example: yellow, yellow-orange, and yellow-green.)

Antiquing: a finish that gives furniture an antique look. Can be purchased in a kit.

Armoire: a large cupboard, originally used in place of a closet: a wardrobe

Battenberg lace: a type of lace originally handmade in Europe. Strips of lace are looped and fastened to make beautiful edgings.

Beveled: an angled cut applied to the outside edges of mirrors or glass

Brocade: a heavy fabric with a woven-in ornate pattern that looks embossed

Café curtains: half curtains, usually attached to a rod by loops or rings

Calico: fabric that has small all-over designs. It is usually made of cotton.

Chintz: a printed and glazed cotton fabric, usually of bright colors.

Complementary colors: two colors that are directly opposite each other on the color wheel

Consignment shops: shops where goods are resold. The goods remain the property of the consigner and can be reclaimed at any point. The shop earns its revenue by taking a percentage of the price.

Cornice: a horizontal molded projection that enhances the design and architecture of a room or building

Cut work: a type of embroider in which the design is outlined in buttonhole stitch. When finished, portions of fabric between the outlining are cut away to create a lacy look.

Damask: a rich, patterned fabric of cotton, linen, or wool

Decoupáge: the technique of decorating a piece with cut out pictures. The pictures are covered with many layers of thin lacquer or varnish.

Delft: a type of pottery made in the city of Delft, Holland

Dhurries: woven rugs made in the far east. The colors are often pastel.

Double dowel joints: joints held together with two pegs or "dowels."

Dotted Swiss: fabric that has tiny dots woven in

Dovetail joints: fan-tailed tenons that interlock at the corners of drawers. Dovetail joints give strength to a piece and increase its value.

Drexel: the name of a furniture maker

Duncan Phyfe: a style of furniture in which legs of tables fan out on the floor

Duvet: a covering for a comforter that is like a large pillowcase. Its purpose is to protect the comforter from soil, but it can also become a decorative element.

Eclectic: a decorating style that mixes different styles of furnishing

Étagére: A piece of furniture with open shelves. Usually is quite decorative.

Finials: an ornamental terminating part: the screw top on a lampshade, the topper on a bedpost, the finishing ornamentation on fence posts and the ends of curtain rods

Fiscus tree: a type of indoor plant that has lance-shaped shiny leaves.

Gingham: a yarn-dyed, woven fabric in stripes, checks, plaids, or solid colors. Most often when we speak of gingham, we are thinking of checks.

Greek key design: an angular pattern often in black and white used by ancient Greeks to decorate pottery

Grosgain ribbon: a ribbed fabric strip woven of silk or more often rayon. Because grosgrain does not stretch, it makes an excellent edging and decorative trim.

Half canopy: A bed canopy that is attached to the wall at ceiling height. It extends only partway over the bed.

Hassock: a thick cushion used as a footstool

Hitchcock chairs: A style of furniture often painted black with stenciled designs on the back rail

Hook and loop tape: commonly called Velcro. One side has small loops and the other has small hooks. The tape is useful for joining two pieces of fabric together or fastening fabric to a hard object such as a wall.

Intensity of color: the depth of color

Jabot: an ornamental cascade of fabric most often used as window decoration

Lambrequins: an ornamental window treatment in which fabric is applied to a padded, shaped board that is mounted over the window

Marbling: a decorative finish in which marbling or streaking is applied to a piece to give it the look of marble. Marbling kits are available in paint and craft stores

Moiré: a fabric that has a watered or wavy look

Monochromatic color scheme: various shades of the same color are used throughout a room or house

Mortise and tenon joints: a system of joining wood in which a tenon—an extension on a piece of wood—is fitted into a mortise—a rectangular hole. The tenon is glued in place resulting in a strong piece of furniture.

Motif: a recurrent thematic element. An example of a motif would be the repetition of a patterned stencil all around a room.

Paisley: abstract curved shapes used repeatedly as pattern in fabrics

Parson's table: a rectangular table in which its legs form its four corners

Particle board: a manmade wood in which chips of wood are glued and pressed together to form a strong sheet of material

Pewter: containers made of an alloy of tin and a number of other kinds of metal. Pewter was once called "poor man's silver."

Piping: a decorative trim of binding or cording usually added to seams and edges.

Primary colors: there are three—red, yellow, and blue. All other colors are derived from these three.

Ragging: a decorative process in which a rolled rag dipped in paint glaze is applied to an already painted wall. Rag roller can be purchased at paint stores.

Roman shade: a decorative shade that is a flat piece of fabric when lowered and accordian folds upward when raised

Secondary colors: those colors which are made by mixing equal parts of two primary colors

Slipcovers: loose fitting coverings for upholstered furniture. These are made of sturdy durable fabrics and are currently very popular.

Split complementary colors: color schemes that combine one hue with hues on each side of it. (For example, yellow with red-violet and blue violet.)

Spring tension rods: rods used for curtains, draperies, and shower curtains that are spring loaded. They can be placed between two solid walls or the insides of window sills. No nailing or brackets are required.

Sponging: a decorative paint finish in which a sponge dipped in a glaze is sponged onto the wall in a decorative pattern. Natural sponges of different sizes and textures are available in paint and craft stores.

Stencil: a template with a punched out pattern used for applying a decorative motif to an object. Several stencils may be used to create one motif.

Style: the way in which something is done. It is a quality of individuality expressed in one's actions and talents. In your home, it is the way you express yourself through color choices, decorative items, furniture styles and placement of furniture.

Swags and tails draperies: a system of window toppers using cascades of fabric (jabots) at the sides of the windows and swags of fabric between

Symmetry: a balance of pieces. Often these are matching pieces placed on either side of an object or room, equal in every way.

Tabbed curtains: simple curtains that have loops of fabric at the top. A decorative rod is fed through the loops.

Template: a pattern or a gauge of thin metal or plastic

Tertiary color: a color resulting from the mixing of two secondary colors

Theme: a decorating idea that is carried out throughout a room or house

Ticking: a striped woven fabric that is very durable. It is often used in pillows to contain feathers.

Tones: colors with black added

Tongue and groove joints: a joint made by fitting a tongue on the edge of a board into a matching groove on another board

Toppers: short decorative curtains used at the top of a window, or small table cloths for tables, or covers on beds

Triad color schemes: Any three equidistant colors on the color wheel

Trompe l'oiel: a style of painting that gives the illusion of photography

Tulle: a fine stiff netting of silk, nylon, or rayon

Valance: a window topper that can be pleated, gathered, or straight fabric. Valances can also be made of wood.

Value of color: how dark or light a color is

Vignette: a grouping of related objects to form an artistic display

Endnotes

1. For a peek at Patsy Clairmont's home see her two books, *Tea with Patsy Clairmont* (Ann Arbor, Mich.: Servant Publications, 1997) and *At Home with Patsy Clairmont* (Ann Arbor, Mich.: Servant Publications, 1998).

2. Bartley Antique Reproduction Furniture Kits. Call 1-800-787-2800 for a catalog.

Suggested Reading

For help living on a shoestring, we like these books written by our friends Jonni McCoy and Mary Hunt:

Financially Confident Woman by Mary Hunt, Broadman & Holman Publishers, Nashville, TN, 1996.

Tiptionary by Mary Hunt, Broadman & Holman Publishers, Nashville, TN, 1997.

Debt Proof Your Kids by Mary Hunt, Broadman & Holman Publishers, Nashville, TN, 1998.

Debt Proof Your Holidays by Mary Hunt, Broadman & Holman Publishers, Nashville, TN, 1998.

The Complete Cheapskate by Mary Hunt, Broadman & Holman Publishers, Nashville, TN, 1998.

Frugal Families by Jonni McCoy, Full Quest Press, Imprint of Holly Hall Publications, Inc., 1998.

DATE			

BAKER & TAYLOR